T0020842

PRAISE FOR ALONE TIME

"More and more in the therapy space those of us who treat mental health conditions show that we are like anyone else. We all need alone time to reflect and make necessary changes. People relate to that and find the wisdom in what they read. This is a self-help book that relies on self: you can make a difference in your own life.

The people I treat often ask me when I am going to take time out for myself; to essentially follow my own advice. I can now answer that I am empowered to do so after reading Dr. Geldart's book."

DR. MARK CROSS, PSYCHIATRIST AND AUTHOR, CHANGING MINDS AND ANXIETY

"Dr. Sybil Geldart shares her clinical expertise using case studies and active techniques that show us how to embrace challenges, and the importance of solitude to reflect, self-regulate and quieten our busy lives. By doing so, we can connect with and enjoy the companionship of the person we know best, ourselves."

DR. SILVIA PIGNATA, WELL-BEING, STRESS AND INTERVENTION RESEARCHER, UNIVERSITY OF SOUTH AUSTRALIA

"This timely and engaging book dispels the myth that alone = lonely. Dr. Geldart draws from her extensive experience as a clinician and a teacher to explain why 'alone time' is essential for our mental and physical health. As a researcher and teacher in the field of positive psychology, I appreciate that this book approaches the idea of solitude as something that everyone can benefit from."

DR. JUDY EATON, PROFESSOR, PSYCHOLOGY, WILFRID LAURIER UNIVERSITY, CANADA

"Post-pandemic, Dr. Sybil Geldart highlights the profound benefits of solitude. She masterfully contrasts pandemic-enforced distancing with the Eastern philosophy of voluntary solitude for spiritual growth, emotional regulation, and inner calm. Through her clinical experience and personal narrative, Geldart reveals how solitude fosters self-awareness and overcomes anxiety."

KATHRYN HENDRICK, MA, HEALTH COMMUNICATIONS SPECIALIST

SYBIL GELDART, PhD

ALONE TIME

Embracing
SOLITUDE
for
HEALTH
and
WELL-BEING

ROCKPOOL

A Rockpool book
PO Box 252
Summer Hill
NSW 2130
Australia

rockpoolpublishing.com
Follow us! f ⊙ rockpoolpublishing
Tag your images with #rockpoolpublishing

ISBN: 9781922785695

Published in 2024 by Rockpool Publishing
Copyright text © Sybil Geldart 2024
Copyright design © Rockpool Publishing 2024

Design and typesetting by Sara Lindberg, Rockpool Publishing
Edited by Lisa Macken

 A catalogue record for this
book is available from the
National Library of Australia

Printed and bound in China
10 9 8 7 6 5 4 3 2 1

For Don, whom I remember spent much of his adult life cultivating a serene personal space – which I reckon gave him a satisfying existence. Because of his love for solitude I try not to fear it.

AUTHOR'S NOTE

My family members and friends described in this book gave full permission to have their stories heard. When they are named it is because they personally gave me their approval to do so. All clients from my clinical practice, current and former, who were described throughout this book also gave permission to have their cases shared. To maintain privacy and confidentiality of patients' personal health information the actual names have been changed and identifying information about clients removed. Note that sometimes a case study presented in this book comprised the details of more than one client or was entirely invented in order to illustrate a concept or idea.

CONTENTS

INTRODUCTION

invite you to cultivate personal space and solitude and be happier in life. That's a clear-cut and confident statement, but, wait: did I actually wish for you to be more alone?

As I entice you to embrace solitude, I am keenly aware of these past years' sad reality of unwavering distancing and repeated lockdowns. At the time of writing my bubble of people witnessed the sixth COVID-19 wave affecting schools, workplaces and other public venues. You could say any teachings about carving out *more* alone time might turn you off completely from reading any further, something my 30-year-old daughter solemnly predicted after I casually mentioned the book proposal. She tactfully offered suggestions for a new topic altogether, and it chillingly resembled the humorless attitude of my daughter's beau, her twin flame, who chimed in: "Don't write about the pandemic. After everything we've been through the last three years, nobody wants to hear about social distancing." Not that I paid any heed to her grim-looking face or to the boyfriend's high-raised brows, as you can tell from the book's title.

No: just to be clear, this book is not about the pandemic. It is about securing physical distance and some decent personal space for your own good. However, before you can appreciate the extent to which solitude and quiet is of value to you, first I ask you to contrast it with social isolation. Consider the fact that I live in a nation with the highest level of democracy and individualism, yet America recently took part in global social isolation in the form of quarantine. Social isolation equals stay-at-home orders. It is something we all had to deal with when so-called SARS-CoV-2 first came into human existence.

SOLITUDE DURING TRYING TIMES

Any proper introduction on the power of solitude should begin with a look at the effects of forced distancing, or quarantine. That is to say, we must acknowledge and validate adversity as a first step in the journey of discovery and healing, then we can truly move forward and talk about something positive and helpful – voluntary distancing.

Most readers will have been born after the influenza pandemic of 1918. You probably have little knowledge of the devastation caused by the Spanish flu on public health. Perhaps you have read one or more history books describing the 1918 pandemic but you didn't actually live through it. Fast forward to late 2019 and you saw in real time how fast the coronavirus disease swept harshly into modern life. Now you have lived through a pandemic. I'm going to make a few predictions here:

my guess is you didn't even give a moment's thought to viral epidemics before COVID-19. On top of that, you had no reason to contemplate a global health disaster in *this* century. I qualify that last prediction: it is possible you've already seen the 2011 science-fiction movie *Contagion*, which mind-blowingly foreshadowed the coronavirus state of affairs.

I was not expecting anything like COVID-19; the coronavirus pandemic pulled to bits all I knew to be true. Before the coronavirus encroached our lives I considered myself nonchalant about health and survival. I was caught up in having a decent standard of living and motivated by a vigorous economy, and admit I took daily comforts and delights for granted. No different from the average middle-class person, I suppose. In the blink of an eye all of that changed when the first wave of COVID-19 appeared. Suddenly everyone around the globe needed to shield the body – or at least the delicate respiratory system – from an unruly virus. It meant taking stern steps to protect yourself and your family. You know the drill: put on your own mask before assisting others. Literally. And that was just the start of things.

The pan-*doom*-ic. The nastiness of the coronavirus showed itself by its damaging effects. The need to slow down the transmission of COVID-19 by staying far away from public venues propelled even the most laidback soul into shock. Confusion. Anxiety. Isolation.

> **Do you remember the ways in which quarantine measures affected your life?**
> **How did lockdown affect your family and friends?**
> **How did you cope with the up-and-down waves of Covid cases?**

Perhaps I generalize and assume that everybody was affected badly. Surely plenty of people had bad feelings and unhappy memories. Think about the start of the pandemic for a moment: didn't you feel sadness, nostalgia even, when social events suddenly shut down? My cousin Josie, widowed and living in a condo in metropolitan Toronto, was in utter disbelief with the quietness of downtown life. "It's not what a lively downtown scene ought to look like," she defended. Restaurants, theatres and markets were almost empty, though at one time they were quite the opposite: industrious and prosperous.

The famous Santa Claus parade, ordinarily zigzagging its way through town on a late November Sunday afternoon, was canceled during the pandemic to keep patrons from getting too close to each other. It meant that joyous children and their parents didn't line city streets. Families weren't found huddled together under blankets, nor did onlookers sip hot chocolate from corner cafes waiting for a memorable holiday event. By the tone in her voice I could tell my dear cousin greatly missed watching endearing events such as the parade. Josie longed for social connection of some sort.

I live in the suburbs about an hour and a half from the big city. Harvest funfairs were canceled in my county for two fall seasons counting. If you grew up near farmland you must have a good idea of the importance of country exhibitions for boosting the local economy and strengthening community. Local farm growers depend on annual parties to showcase their hard work: their best maple syrup, their largest pumpkins, their sweetest apple pies. They draw on city folk who, for at least one short season during the entire year, are thankful for the fruits of farm labor. Indeed, for years when my family was young I made a conscious effort every single Labor Day weekend to lead three impressionable youngsters to the fair and display my brood's heartfelt appreciation. However, there was no one to thank in my township when autumn festivals were called off due to the pandemic.

More than just social life was affected by quarantine. Workforce workers moved from office to remote work. Students switched from the bricks and mortar classroom to personal home computers and virtual classes. Perhaps you belong in one of these vocations: office worker, college student, webinar trainee, caregiver or perhaps the spouse of a learner. Maybe you spent more time than you imagined possible dividing home and office items, configuring household furniture and learning to use technology properly. When all this was finally resolved, next was the burdensome task of finding an ounce of free time to sit quietly in work mode. Even if you had stamina to perform, it might have been tricky without the support from peers, special tools or high-speed internet. The job was compounded when, at the same time, you needed to care for significant others such as young children, an elderly parent, your beloved family dog or the standoffish cat.

Listen, I know how you feel about the harsh by-products of our pandemic. It hit me hard and fast in all the ways just described. I flip-flopped with emotions: one day just loving getting caught up in errands, trying out recipes and taking blissful walks in my neighborhood, but the next day feeling bored, lonely and pining for joyful visits to the local shopping mall. I really missed hanging out with friends. Truth be told, I even missed people whom I didn't really care about until they stopped being in my sphere as a result of the pandemic. Extreme reactions are what I lived with. What a crazy time.

On a grave note, the fallout of the pandemic affected me badly. I sorely missed the chance to be with my father when he passed in 2020. The hospital minimized compassionate visits, allowing just half an hour of time with his wife, my mother. As his only offspring, I sat alone in the hospital parking lot while a sympathetic nurse from inside the building offered me an iPad to see my dying parent in virtual mode. It was a kind gesture all things considered, but it was a useless solution. My dad was in no condition to partake in a video exchange at his deathbed. And, of course, our facetime – mine from my parents' SUV and his from the palliative care ward – was frustrating to say the least. Who would ever have guessed we would be saying final goodbyes this way? In all the years I have known the old man I never envisioned being forced to stay away when it was his time to depart this life. Along with grief, I was irritated with hospital nurses for enforcing new Covid-related policies. I was distraught with COVID-19 for making my father die alone and making my loss excruciating and surreal.

THE UPSIDE OF SOLITUDE

I brought up the pandemic and its ill effects so you can appreciate the difference between worldwide enforced distancing and what all of us should be aiming for: *voluntary* distancing. I wanted to showcase the antithesis between mandated solitude and voluntary personal space. The idea that personal space and distancing serve some good in this universe is not a new one. Practicing solitude has been wholeheartedly welcomed in Eastern traditions over time without end, wherein its purpose is to elicit self-reflection, gain self-knowledge and seek a better understanding of the world. It is for this reason that this book, *Alone Time,* taps into some well-known, modernized Buddhist-driven practices. Strategies and practical tips will help you understand your place in this world. Best of all, it will make you acknowledge your boundless potential.

That some solitude would be good for me personally struck me smack in the center of the forehead when, pandemic chaos aside, I saw that it was quieting, informative and not at all as scary as I had thought it would be. Doing my job in the absence of comrades and co-workers was mandatory at the start of the pandemic. Like other office employees I scrambled to move a boxful of belongings from the workplace office to a home office, a switch that caused a radical change in how I conducted my duties, both as a professor and as a therapist. I worried about how I and my students and clients would adapt.

The good news is that I managed the move to remote work better than expected, and even the most reluctant of clients adapted to teletherapy. What a relief! We all made it: we survived social distancing and the chain of technical issues that came with brand new e-tasks. I've been doing the Zoom thing for more than three years now – you could say I'm a Zoom virtuoso – and so have a great number of my students and clients mastered the new platform. More than that, I discovered mighty nice perks of doing work from home: dodging travel time and winter driving, saving costs from rising petrol prices, avoiding expensive purchases of dressy suits, skirts and designer shoes (whoever would notice the bottom attire on video calls anyway?) and being flexible and more available to my people and furry friends who need me on pretty short notice.

Being alone at home in the absence of social connections and external stimulation did more than just offer a number of practical benefits. It also meant that I necessarily paid less attention to the external world and closer attention to my inner thoughts and feelings. When I say that solitude has the effect of quieting the mind, what I mean is that it quickly changed how my emotions were experienced. In other words, without anyone advising me to do so I was able to take note of some very strong feelings such as fear, anxiety and sadness. We all recognize that fear and anxiety can take a pretty strong hold on the internal, physiological state. By paying more attention to high-arousal emotions it gave me the chance to gain control and actually begin to lower intense physiological arousal. What I described for myself about learning to lessen strong feelings of anxiety and sadness in the absence of outside stimulation has been backed up by research. Therefore, some solitude in your own life will bring you a range of benefits that you can discover on your own.

* * *

I asked myself whether a self-help book would be a worthwhile contribution to readers. After all, there are thousands of self-help guides available on the market. Books published 20 to 30 years ago beat me to the punch and advised lofty consumers and workaholics on why they should welcome more repose in life. Contemporary books teach otherwise inhibited folks the underrated benefits of introversion, introspection and independent thinking. In other words, there's a lot out there already on the power of self-determination and mindfulness. From what I researched, though, not one self-help book has dealt with the relevance of personal space in a changing world.

The reality is that, for quite some time now, all of us have been living in a fast-changing world. Technology is moving along at a furious pace, too high-speed for baby boomers such as myself. Please know this kids: your elders are struggling with tech. People are multitasking, having difficulty focusing on one important thing at a time and trying to keep up with a barrage of stimulation and demands coming from all angles and places. And, regardless of age and status, every person on earth is grappling with trying times one way or another: supply-chain shortages, high inflation, and the idea of brand-new coronavirus variants disturbing people's notions of global health and safety.

What I have gained over years of education, mental health training and lived experience is what I put forward in this book so that you can start living well in a changing world. First off, I am a mother: a devoted one at that. Second, I took too many years to count to ultimately become an *expert*, a professor of psychology. Years of caregiving, combined with scholarly research in child development not to mention numerous trials and errors, kept my significant others nicely treading above water and thriving.

I am also a registered psychologist trained in cognitive behavioral therapy and third-wave therapies. I work tirelessly with children, adolescents and adults. I help individuals and families and people of diverse backgrounds with diverse matters. Students who come to hear my lectures and clients who seek counseling know well enough the importance I place on private space. I depend on it to help me and my people work comfortably on issues together. I promote well-being by practicing mindfulness and acceptance and by teaching clients and students the value of reflection and calm. Advice shared heartedly with my followers can be summed up as follows:

- **_You_** can change how you feel by changing the way you think about people and things.
- **_You_** can improve your mood by eliminating unhelpful behaviors and starting healthy ones.
- **_You_** can accept adversity as being a normal part of the life course yet remain strong and hopeful.

These words ought to be conveyed not only to those who wrestle with mental health concerns but to everybody reading this now – a reminder that positive change originates from within. *You* can change yourself.

In the above three statements of wisdom, did you catch the word "You" in bold and italics? I want *you* to discover optimal strategies and practical tools to bring on positive thinking and better health. Sitting right before you, not too difficult to enrich, is your personal space. Personal space, or solitude, sets your mind to rest point and helps you think clearly about how to manage important tasks and sometimes difficult issues. It is paramount in a changing world.

Keep in mind that in this book I make a whole lot of recommendations via example: personal anecdotes, clinical case studies and empirical data in the scientific field of psychology. This way you will absorb ideas from various sources and more easily link them to your own life experiences as you see fit. If you're a social worker, therapist or a friend of someone who you believe is in need of support, take advantage of the strategies in this book to help improve the other person's quality of life. If you're an educator with a passion for learning in spite of fast-changing technology, apply the material to foster good learning strategies in your pupils. In striving to help a loved one, parents and grandparents will benefit as well. Family has both devotion and resolve to tackle challenging situations faced by young people today. Sometimes you just need a point in the right direction. Maybe all you need is encouragement.

Personal space is worth it despite how much or how little outside stimulation you are accustomed to. Are you an outgoing soul? Do you happily gravitate towards comrades and gregarious events? If you are socially inclined then I fully understand how hard it must have been turning your back on fun gatherings during lockdown. Being a social butterfly myself, I appreciate how awkward it was to choose a distant wave and pantomimed big hug over tight bear hugs, firm high fives and warm kisses. Recall that this is what we had to do to circumvent transmitting the coronavirus. That was before, but even now you will see that there is a silver lining in embracing some alone time.

On the flip side, you might see yourself not as the outgoing type but as introverted in character. A shy person. For all I know, solitude may already be your beloved way of life. My point is: time alone allows you to take a slower, deliberate pace and explore inner strengths, set goals and overcome problems. It allows you to connect mind and body and connect your being with the outside world in a less daunting way.

This book gives a nod to the marvelous goal of self-improvement. You picked it up, so something tells me you have hope for a better future. Maybe it is your personality, know-how and luck even to use whatever means to remain resilient during trying times such as the ones recently experienced by all of us, and the ones that are ongoing.

HOW TO USE THIS BOOK

Take a look at what is covered in this self-help guide. Chapter 1 helps you see what can be gained in your life by voluntary distancing and personal space. Chapter 2 details the concept of personal space: you will discover what personal space could look like for you. Chapter 3 highlights what distancing should not entail and when, instead, it may be optimal to enlist professional help. From Chapter 4 onwards you will learn to use your personal space effortlessly to help you in diverse ways – sometimes in profound ways.

The techniques outlined in chapters 4 to 7 activate your body and mind and improve your physical and mental health and your well-being. Physical exercise at home, monitoring and altering daily activities and mood, crafting and self-expression will make you healthy and happier. No more relying on public venues or other people to make you energized and satisfied with life. Rather, if it is your will you can use personal skills and self-soothing tools to improve you . . . by yourself.

Chapter 8 introduces the concept of mindfulness and techniques to bring about self-reflection and calm. Chapter 9 asks you to be grateful via methods such as crafting a letter of gratitude, using a happiness journal and practicing meditation to keep you centered on the here and now and allow you to accept present situations as they are. Chapters 10 and 11 focus on methods to better manage the painful experiences of anxiety, panic and other strong emotions. Emotion regulation is needed when life gets chaotic and unmanageable.

Once you gain new and wonderful ways to cultivate personal space for enhancing health and wellness, next consider how you would persist in seeking solitude into the future. To give you an example, alone time to complete work and schooling has become commonplace these days; now, more than ever, employees are doing job duties remotely. Chapter 12 shows you how to make a comfortable home base for work and how to create work-life boundaries, build in home ergonomics and develop other skills. These strategies, in turn, will make you satisfied and productive, and what businesses would *not* wish their employees to be both satisfied on the job and more productive? Chapter 13 offers tools for creating a home office for learning – whether you are a student, professional in training or lifelong learner. Remote learning is valuable in modern-day life because it makes you an independent learner. Be prepared to be active in your own learning.

Chapter 14 shifts gears from learning to extracurricular activities and asks you to persist in your fitness and nutritional goals. On the topic of exercise and body health, be cautious of social media influencers and be sure to seek trustworthy role models.

I recommend you read all of the chapters and strongly suggest you take in all the ways that personal space and solitude positively influence diverse areas of life you might not have considered before. However, there is no specific order in which to read this material: it is a journey for yourself and you may decide to read about overcoming anxiety or depression before tackling regular exercise or how to express yourself via crafts and hobbies. In the final chapter, Chapter 15, take the time to review strategies, practical tips and skills to enable success in work, school and home life. Analyze the methods and strategies to maintain space and solitude going forward but, first, find a good reason to want to be alone – at least some of the time. Chapter 1 explains what I mean by that.

PART 1

P
R
E
P
A
R
E

SOLITUDE: THE KEY TO A HAPPIER LIFE

I don't want to be alone . . .
I want to be left alone.

– LEGENDARY HOLLYWOOD ACTRESS AUDREY HEPBURN

The goal here is *wanting to distance yourself,* for a bit of time anyway. Do it for its positive effects. I would not have taken the time to write about the importance of solitude if I did not believe that the act of voluntary distancing has benefits in your life: in your profession; in being educated, trained or retrained; and, most of all, in being emotionally healthy and inspired in terms of life goals and desires for the future. The contents of this book will guide you through all of those benefits. First, you need to be in the loop and know what is so downright good about being in solitude.

> **Can you think of good reasons
> to spend time alone?
> Why say that solitude is the
> key to a happier life?**

For many people it is hard to think of good reasons to spend more time alone. In general, people of all ages tend to carry negative thoughts and feelings about distancing and solitude. I have done so in the past, and I wouldn't be surprised if you too have had negative perceptions of purposefully being alone. In modern Western society, being in the presence of other people is the norm.

It's what we do in all facets of life: work, leisure and so on. Not having people around us might make us look as though we have been rejected or isolated from the social group. The idea that someone deliberately wants to be separate from others can give the impression that they are somehow abnormal or weird compared with other people, and maybe unhappy or depressed. It is fascinating that we all learn to become social and to value social connections from a very young age.

Given the emphasis on social connectivity, do you personally have any of these perceptions about spending more time alone?

COMMON PERCEPTIONS ABOUT BEING IN SOLITUDE
Loneliness
Unhappiness
Vulnerability to painful memories
Feelings of distress
Isolation
Rejection

Solitude is often seen as something negative, but it should be seen as something positive. Despite the negative connotation of solitude, there is in fact much value in being alone. Let's see why. Read below and you will see that some solitude and quiet will bring on self-awareness, independent thinking and more positive thinking. Ironically, solitude can make you feel more emotionally connected to other people rather than make you feel separate or disconnected, which is what a lot of people assume happens when they are away from the crowd.

SOLITUDE DOES NOT KEEP YOU DISCONNECTED

Think about this: you can be in a room full of friends and loving family members yet feel lonely, sad and highly anxious or agitated. Therefore, it is not accurate to assume or profess that loneliness equals being alone.

It is tempting to see distancing and connectedness as polar opposites or two ends of a spectrum because being detached from the outside world might result in you being disconnected from others, but being alone and being lonely are not one and the same. Making yourself stay alone for a short period of time indicates you have consciously decided to distance yourself from outside stimulation. It is a deliberate action on your part to stay grounded within yourself and let external forces slip away, and it is a positive behavior intended to bring about positive outcomes.

You can feel connected emotionally to other beings even while detaching yourself from social events. Feeling connected is a mental representation we hold about ourselves in relation to our world. This mental presentation is called "schema" by cognitive psychologists. Being connected is having the schema or sense of belonging to a community. Feeling connected with yourself implies self-acceptance and self-love, and involves an integration between the mind and bodily sensations. The late Armand DiMele, radio broadcaster, psychotherapist and founder of The Positive Mind Center in New York, said it like this: "When people go within and connect with themselves, they realize they are connected to the universe and they are connected to all living things."

It has long been known that without social connectedness, physical and psychological symptoms can result. Depression, anxiety and overall poor emotional health can happen when we become isolated emotionally. A range of physical problems can occur as well, such as having high blood pressure and disrupted sleep. However, the benefit of voluntarily distancing ourselves from others, at least every so often, is that we end up improving connectedness with ourselves as well as with other people. Always know that having a positive and healthy connection with the social world is possible despite being physically separate from other beings for short periods of time.

> Being connected with other beings is
> important for good emotional health.
> You can remain connected even when, every
> so often, you detach from social events.

SOLITUDE AND SELF-AWARENESS

Purposefully separating yourself from other people gives you an opportunity to look carefully within. Being alone gives you the chance to think about yourself and your needs and goals without undue pressure, distractions or interference. You might agree with what I just said but then turn around and tell me you are way too busy right now to make time for yourself. I get it: your calendar is already full and your mind is overloaded with important things to do. I've been there, trust me. Let me repeat: taking time to be on your own and think about you – and no one else – is vital for personal growth.

When you voluntarily distance yourself from outside stimulation and the multitude of forces that surround your being you truly get to know who you are and where you want to be. I like to remind us all that we live in a fast-paced society, and that because of this it is easy to get caught up with the external world and learn how to make things happen efficiently and effortlessly. The faster things get done the more we can take on next time, and the more automatic thinking becomes. All of these actions are commonplace in a break-neck, highly stimulating world but now is the time to put on the brakes, to slow things right down. In the presence of some private space away from the hustle and bustle of everyday life you will find it easier to think about personal goals and decide whether you are anywhere close to achieving them. You will be more self-aware, and the bonus is that you can change your current goals and path in your life course so you become happier and more satisfied. Just face it: if you happen to be a busy person like I am then the more you *need* some alone time.

SOLITUDE AND INDEPENDENT THINKING

It is obvious to say but I will do it anyway: you've lived with yourself your entire life, and because of this you ought to know yourself better than anyone else. Sometimes it is good to be on your own and make decisions for yourself without being influenced by other people. I realize it is not always easy being independent and confident in your own decision-making, especially in a digital era of constant connectivity. Besides, we live in a business world where productive think-tanks and non-hierarchical group problem solving are encouraged in the workplace. Group effort is pushed even before the start of a career as high school teachers and college instructors teach us the power of collaborative decision-making and wholesome solidarity and teamwork. Being with others, working with others and learning from others is prized, but that doesn't mean you can't do things independently or think things in a unique way for your own good.

I used to be terribly uncomfortable doing things alone and figuring things out on my own. As an only child, I was raised by devoted parents and an over-attentive, Italian-speaking grandmother hovering over me every waking minute. It was suffocating receiving constant protection and direction, yet thoughtful and heavenly at the same time. Not surprisingly, I grew up having difficulty making it on my own. I relied on steadfast emotional support from la familia. Even now I find myself uneasy – mentally lost, actually – when physically separated from the faithful cell phone, unfailing social media and friendly social support. I'm sure you've had one or more moments of panic when you've realized you left the device at home or in the car and suddenly found yourself turning in the opposite direction to retrieve the almighty phone. It turns out that we touch our mobile devices more than 2,600 times per day.

> *In order to be open to creativity,*
> *one must have the capacity for*
> *constructive use of solitude. One must*
> *overcome the fear of being alone.*

– EXISTENTIAL PSYCHOLOGIST ROLLO MAY

Let it be known that I have in fact slammed on the brakes when it comes to a perpetual need for connection to people and things. I now realize every day that alone time gives me an excellent opportunity to look within and improve thy self, and I make more effort to ignore the social atmosphere of present-day living. This might have been painstaking for me at one time in my life, but now I can honestly say I deliberately place my much-cherished iPhone on a charger in my study while I cook, watch television and, yes, even do my laundry too entirely depossessed by my contacts and their undertakings. Having practiced solitude and seen the positive outcomes for me personally, I no longer fear being alone and staying grounded with myself. It is worth every bit of time I have with myself to figure out who I am and what this world is all about. I profess this with emphasis: *a time and place to reflect and rest is in your best interest.*

SOLITUDE ELIMINATES MIND CHATTER

Looking within yourself does not always or immediately spark warm and fuzzy feelings. By looking at your situtions from past lived experiences and your enduring personality traits – good and bad – you surely run the risk of being vulnerable to some personal faults. You may start to mentally confront nagging problems that won't go away even though you had successfully ignored snags and crises up until now. If you are currently going through an exceptional circumstance, then sitting alone in your thoughts may conjure up painful memories and make you feel crappy about past actions and events and the people in your life.

Take some time to understand what is going on whenever you give in to unwanted mind chatter. It is like the mind has a habit of replaying recent conversations, particularly very unhappy exchanges or scenes, over and over again: the events of a weekend party, the happenings in a business meeting, the dialogue you just had with a relative or friend. Negative thoughts swirl and repeat at the end of a busy day. Ruminating thoughts are rampant at bedtime. Bedtime is a down time when your body and mind are turning away outside stimulation to get ready for rest, but before sleep sets in all that is left is unhealthy mind chatter.

Have you thought these words in the past?

- I can't turn off my brain.
- I'm always in my head.
- I overthink things.
- I have racing thoughts.

Persistent negative thoughts restrict your ability to focus and hinder you from making good decisions. Be aware of when your mind is caught up in ruminations, but don't stop there. Understand you have power to control negative thinking, that you are capable of abolishing mind chatter. What I am proposing here is that solitude – if practiced using mindfulness and a non-judgemental approach – will eliminate mind chatter, not make it worse. The key is to understand what solitude is about. In a nutshell, acquiring some personal space and solitude will help you become mindful.

Mindfulness is an important theme running through various topics in this book. By using mindfulness methods you will consciously move your attention from a bad thought to a better one. You will become practiced at shifting your mind away from intrusive, distressing thoughts towards more pleasant ones. I bet you will learn to do this quickly, especially if you agree to practice and especially if you find and use your personal space. And, remember, you have free will, which is the first step towards changing the way you see things in life. You can decide to use mental space for positive thinking, not ruminating, which will require embracing time alone so you can pay closer attention to your thinking processes.

EMBRACING ALONE TIME DESPITE THE SHIFTING BOTTOM

I want to introduce you to other advantages of enriching solitude and personal space in order to live well.

I am a believer that some personal space and solitude, when initiated by you, helps you thrive given today's landscape. Remote work, self-learning strategies and emotion-regulation skills are all necessary to manage life in a changing world. Perhaps you find yourself struggling with caregiving responsibilities, or possibly financial burdens. Maybe you recognize you are missing much-needed coping skills, or wish you were not so worried about things and were more forward thinking and confident in what you do. With personal space you will discover life skills that will assist if or when you feel trapped in difficult circumstances.

The contents of this book will move you to that better space and will help you develop the skills and good attitude that are vital in today's world. Examples of skills include:

- learning to adapt to change
- staying in tune with your emotions and body sensations
- finding a work/life balance
- using technology wisely
- organizing your time and materials to be productive
- promoting physical exercise, safety and creativity.

It may sound counterintuitive, maybe absurd, that I am pushing you to look for quiet space – doing it solo, so to speak, at a time when social distancing has been a big part of pandemic life. Social distancing is still inescapable at times, and it is wise to try to live normally without absolute fear of possible quarantine in the future. Remember that just when we thought breakthrough vaccines would save citizens from infection, the next thing we saw was that subvariants were lurking and defying health authorities' efforts to control the unruly contagion. When will worldwide virulent disease come to an end or, at least, when will future plagues be terminated quickly, and what can you do for yourself to maintain good health and sanity?

It's not only global health concerns that are troublesome. Many children frantically turn to their open-hearted helicopter parents for guidance and unfailing support. Many of today's teens feel utterly immobilized when navigating high school and social life. Young adults are career bound and optimistic while fighting the rising costs of home ownership and hefty mortgage loans. Couples are hopeful yet stressed, striving for high-paying jobs with the expectation they will one day lay a fine roof firmly over the family unit's head. When will gas prices go down? How about toilet paper costs? Consider this simple yet mystifying question from a single mother with three emerging adult children: is the current buying trend insane or what?

Because of the shifting bottom it is no wonder you may be searching for ways to adapt to the (constantly changing) new normal. At this moment you may not know the best way to take charge of life again, so I want to give you meaningful and appropriate ways to do just that. The bottom line is that you will need distancing and personal space if you want to take hold of yourself and your circle and live well.

You may be wondering how to achieve or create personal space, so let's find out how to spawn a personal space.

CHAPTER 2

SPAWN A PERSONAL SPACE

The quieter you become the more you are able to hear.

– SPIRITUAL LEADER AND
PSYCHOLOGIST RAM DASS

Sometimes personal space is conceptualized as an invisible bubble during face-to-face conversation. The study of this type of personal space is known as "proxemics" and is an example of what I *don't* mean when I refer to "personal space" in this book. What exactly is proxemics? It is a perfectly understood space that each of two people occupies while having a typical back-and-forth dialogue. We learn about it in childhood, though we never actually measure the distance with a ruler or think about it consciously.

Let's look at an example of you and I facing each other in casual talk: no doubt we would stand anywhere from 3 to 10 feet apart, a value set according to North American customs (although note that exact values vary across cultures). How far apart we are from one another is intended to respect boundaries and not overstep any one person's comfort zone, but if suddenly I were to step in a tad closer – say, 1 to 1.5 feet away from your face – you might feel weird about the closeness. I just invaded your space. According to social etiquette rules, approximately 1 to 3 feet between people should be reserved for those who know each other well and are comfortable with nearness; that is, romantic couples and family members. Personal space helps each person in the social exchange feel protected and safe.

The personal space I am asking you to create is the same as the invisible bubble insofar as it is designed to make you feel comfortable and safe. It is the same in that you will end up with some physical distance between you and other people. However, when I talk about personal space in this book it is more complex than the invisible bubble surrounding you during conversation. It is multifaceted, having more than one side or layer. On the one hand, your personal space can exist in a separate place or entity: a retreat tucked away somewhere for privacy and quiet. On the other hand, personal space comprises internal space within your mind to reflect and be at peace. I will expand here on my definitions of physical (material) space and internal (mental) space.

Physical space = material space
(a summer house, study, outdoor patio, cottage dock)

Internal space = mental space
(the mind, intelligent thinking, emotional expression)

MATERIAL SPACE

There are many ways to describe physical space: envision green space; think of a private haven with old cypress trees and botanical gardens; or imagine an oceanic site or seascape. Some may be fortunate to escape the routines of life by owning a summer house in Greece overlooking the Mediterranean Sea, a loft home on the exquisite Caribbean island of Belize, a snowbird's condo in sunny Florida or a rustic cottage in Canada's true north. Picturesque villas and serene vacation homes are splendid. Who wouldn't want this kind of retreat to better themselves? These are perfect examples of places for unwinding, taking pleasure in something new and seeing the things around you in a different light.

Who are we kidding? These serene spaces are not accessible to the majority. Having another home away from a primary home is expensive to run; it is not likely that the average person can own a vacation condo or villa. Does this mean you must be rich or lucky in order to achieve that perfect space? Not at all.

A remote oasis is not necessary for you to create an effective personal space. On the contrary, try to imagine a room or spot in your home that offers tranquility and warm vibes. It might be an endearing place that evolved as a sanctuary over time. Maybe it was specially designed by you for quiet thinking. It might be outdoors on the patio, a place to connect with the earth that contains a garden, bird bath, sun and blue sky and fresh air or a breeze. Think about this:

- What is the purpose of having your own private space?
- What materials might you need to make your perfect place a reality?

THREE PERSONAL SPACES

Let me share three unique spaces created by my contacts Jalysa, Amir and Dale. Each space happened to work well to meet the needs of their holder but none were expensive to make or difficult to rustle up.

JALYSA'S MINI HAVEN

Jalysa is a 30-year-old millennial, a junior lawyer renting a 560 square feet condo near her firm. She devotes long hours to legal cases, which means working both at the office and home. It is crammed at Jalysa's place. A kitchen island serves as a breakfast nook and desk, living room shelves as a law library and the guestroom – with bed, dresser and lamp – as sleeping quarters and a copier room.

Despite its micro size, Jalysa separated a 5 x 6 feet area near the sliding doors and added real plants, aromatherapy candles, two toss pillows and a mat. There she practices yoga and, when doing so, she makes sure there is no interference from books, file folders or a ringing iPhone. You could say Jalysa created a mini haven to balance demanding work and life.

AMIR'S LOFT

Amir needed to separate school and social life. He is a Gen-Z college student sharing a Victorian house with four 20 year olds. His study was located close to common areas such as the kitchen and living room. The frat boys loved to host parties, but Amir (not to mention his parents) worried that the noise and fun would interfere with him completing gruelling math courses.

Amir used some muscle, creativity and a few bucks to find solitude within the last-century house. His roommates helped clear out the upstairs loft so Amir could settle in with his computer, workstation and bedroom furniture. Amir's father inserted a glass French door at the top of the stairwell to bring in natural light and keep him connected with the rest of the household. Noise-cancelling headphones helped with focus. The move was successful, and school is more successful. Amir happily drops in to socialize with the guys, but only on his terms and when he's ready to take a break from challenging schoolwork.

DALE'S TRAVEL TOTE

Dale is neither a student nor office worker: he is a baby boomer, a photographer who travels quite a bit in the USA and UK for modelling photo shoots. Time away from home base interferred with things he liked to do; for example, he had an interest in running.

His desire was to run every morning, not just when he was back at the townhouse in the suburbs. It occurred to Dale that to create an exercise routine, any special space for exercise had to be mobile and had to be able to go with him while traveling. He came up with a plan: when he packed his travel bag Dale included a special tote with a favorite tracksuit, sneakers, water bottle and ear buds. He used these items for a morning run no matter where he was stationed and he added a playlist on his phone that he updated from time to time. This collection of items helped Dale achieve fitness goals, which made him happy.

If you're imagining spaces like these ones, ask yourself what you plan to use the space for.

MENTAL SPACE

So far I have defined personal space as having physical dimensions, be it at home or on the road if that is your liking. Personal space represents more than just a physical entity.

The mind is a precious mechanism that is still poorly understood by scientists. However, we do know that the mind represents an internal place to reflect and problem solve. Mental space is never empty. Cognitive psychologists who study human thought and intelligence have discovered something interesting about the adult mind: it produces thousands of thoughts each day. That sure is a lot of thinking from morning to sunset.

*Life consists in what a man
is thinking of all day.*

— ESSAYIST RALPH WALDO EMERSON

As suggested by this quote, we end up doing things and living a certain way just by how we think about events and people all day long. With all of this thinking it is helpful to have an internal sense of breathing space in order to organize your thoughts, re-evaluate situations and decompress. Personal space can bring the mind to rest point, which helps you think more clearly about how to manage difficult issues. It has a rippling effect: no longer clouded by negative emotions and poor focus, it is possible to make good decisions. With good decisions come positive thoughts, a feeling of relief, a feeling of joy. Buddhist philosophers and modern theorists all agree that a small portion of time alone to self-analyze is downright good for your emotional health.

Let's review physical space and mental space. Take a few minutes to find a quiet physical place such as the quiet room where you have been reading this book. Be seated comfortably and close your eyes if this helps you connect with your mental space, but before shutting your eyes read the following tip for consciously exploring your mind.

TIP: BEING CONSCIOUS OF YOUR MENTAL SPACE

Realize that the mind naturally wanders – as it should, as there is nothing wrong with having constant mental activity. Even with the wandering of thoughts it is possible for you to take charge and deliberately move your focus to something in particular. Go ahead now and gently shift your attention to one single thought or one point of focus. You can choose what you want your focus to be on, but here are some examples:

- attend to your breathing
- focus on someone in your life
- listen to a sound you hear outside.

**What would you like to make
your point of focus?**

As you focus on one object or entity in your
mind notice that at times your mind tries to
think about something entirely different.
Whenever you find your mind moving
from where you want it to be, gently bring
it back to the focus of interest. I cannot
stress this enough: be prepared to gently
redirect attention more than once or even
many times. This is normal. Each time you
do things to keep your focus on the present
moment you are practicing mindfulness.

In practicing mindfulness you will observe your own thoughts and notice patterns in thinking and behaviors. You will discover that changing the smallest things will improve your mood. You will have the chance to try mindfulness techniques in the chapters that follow.

This is a good time for a summary of why it is good to have mental space. Turning to a personal space for quiet and reflection reduces anxious distress and other negative feelings, and leads to smarter thinking and feeling better. I liken the process to this simple flow chart:

Personal space → *(leads to) Mind at rest point*
→ *Clear(er) thinking, feeling good*

Some personal space may be needed just for you, or it may be for the benefit of a special person you know who is struggling with some aspect of their life. I advise you or the friend to turn to the privacy of the household. If possible, make the homestead a personal headquarters to reflect, self-learn and problem solve. Naturally, only you can decide what a comfortable space looks like. Remember, personal space need not be restricted to a faraway villa or loft. It can be what and where you want it to be and it can be portable and flexible.

Personal space can help a lot. It can make us mindful, restful, creative and productive among other positive outcomes. From Chapter 4 onwards I will show you how to use personal space to activate your body and mind, manage strong feelings, improve job performance, make learning and school easier and boost your leisure life, but first we need to take some precautions. Chapter 3 outlines how we need to be clear about what distancing or alone time should *not* be.

C
H
A
P
T
E
R
—
3

WHAT DISTANCING
SHOULD
NOT BE

*Each of us is now electronically connected
to the globe, and yet we feel utterly alone.*

– DAN BROWN, AUTHOR OF *ANGELS & DEMONS*

Humans are social animals. Each of us depends on others to survive: we rely on kinfolk, clan, tribe, family … at least to some extent. We need people for aid, growth and companionship. Even if you are no socialite, I presume you have significant people within your circle to whom you feel a bond. To feel wanted, loved and accepted is a basic human need. The need for love and belonging – friendship, family, intimacy, a sense of connection – is a strong human motivation and is smack in the middle of Maslow's hierarchy of needs, proposed in 1943.

Remember that distancing ought to be about willingly separating from your social group. It is viewed entirely as a positive behavior and is expected to be undertaken voluntarily. The opposite to that is strict or involuntary distancing, an asocial behavior that can bring on isolation and depression. Solitude should never be forced upon you; you should never feel obligated to separate yourself from others when it does not feel right or when it is not what you want.

Aloneness should not be too frequent either and should not take up the majority of your day. For some people, being alone literally translates into spending the majority of their time in front of a computer monitor or a smartphone. Statistics show that the average adult spends more than six to eight hours per day using the internet and social media. A heavy internet user spends almost three times that amount of time, about 16 hours per day. That is a lot of screen time! It sure wouldn't be healthy if you checked out from the outside world and centered your life on online gaming, video streaming and other forms of social media. Playing video games and scrolling newsfeeds are highly addictive behaviors. A considerable amount of recent research highlights the grave effects of steady internet use, which has been linked to a number of health problems – namely, social isolation, depression, obesity and social anxiety.

If you do find yourself glued to a device and persistently leave behind friends and family to be online, then it sounds like you are obsessed with the virtual world. The virtual world is your life. If you make every possible excuse to avoid work, hanging with your crowd or spending time with your children and partner then it sounds like you cannot separate real and virtual worlds. If this is true for you, take a moment right now to consider its negative effects as you are very likely neglecting some pretty darn important things in life. Ask yourself these questions:

Ǫ Am I spending a lot of time scrolling feeds and sites on the internet?

○ Are people in my life spending too much time on their device?

○ Do I get anxious when I don't have my phone on me? Do I notice loved ones distressed when they forget to bring their device with them?

○ Am I pushing away work and friendly gatherings just to be on my phone?

If you answered "Yes" to any of these questions you may be overusing the internet at the cost of healthy behaviors. I suggest you go over the questions a second time and answer them in reference to someone special in your life, maybe your partner or a youngster. Do you notice that your loved ones seem to be overusing the internet and social media?

It is necessary to turn off devices: on occasion. If turning off your cell phone is hard to imagine let alone actually do, then consider muting the sound as the first step. Go one step further and push your phone out of the way – at more than arm's reach. Do it now, actually.

To get the most out of this reading you should give an emphatic "No!" to multitasking. What I mean is, you should avoid looking at endless text messages and emails while reading this content. Think about it for a minute: if your goal is to be successful and happier by learning strategies and helpful tips then you will need to concentrate on the book and not be distracted by other information.

> **Be engaged and actively involved
> in the here and now.**

Separating yourself from electronic devices is necessary in order to stay mindful, and the exercises in this book will make you conscious of essential things you have been ignoring or missing out on. Mindfulness comes up under several topics, with an emphasis in Chapter 8.

WHY DISTANCING IS NECESSARY TO MINIMIZE HARM

Sometimes there is no question about the need to retreat and be separated from others. Think about whether you have ever said these words: "Back off, I need space." It sounds as though you might have been annoyed, disappointed or hurt about a situation or person. It is hard to think clearly when someone is doing things to make you feel bad and refuses to let up, so it's better to focus on resolving the issue without persistent negativity nagging at you. Be on your own momentarily rather than being sidetracked by someone else's harmful words.

It is not rude if you move away from an escalating situation; don't get manipulated by the actions of others. When there is the potential for aggressive behavior, real or imagined, your body will react by either charging forward in an equally aggressive state to win the fight or by stepping back when winning is not likely. Distancing keeps you protected whenever there is a potential for harm.

Even with no actual threat of violence your body will naturally withdraw from hostility for survival, but be careful that you are not letting yourself indefinitely retreat into silence. Eventually you will need to get to the root of the problem. Use your private space to think things through and take action to improve adversive situations.

We've been talking about you being the victim and needing personal space for your safety and health, but what if you are the person inflicting harm? If you are the aggressor – the person who is angry, hostile or bitter – then everyone else in harm's way needs protection. The person being harmed needs to keep safely away from you, and you definitely need to back off. Oftentimes it is harder to distance yourself when you are on the offence. What does it mean to be on the attack? Maybe you are trying to make a point, say the last words, be in control and so forth, or maybe something inside pushes you so that you don't back down and let things go. If you do not back away you will end up feeling worse. You might end up with guilt and shame for nasty words and inappropriate behaviors and eventually you'll be unhappy with your aggressive reactions.

Suppose you are having trouble letting go of intense anger and making it hard to give someone their much-needed personal space. Try these quick actions:

- ♎ Do not react; calm down.
- ♎ Immediately step away from a highly charged situation.

I understand that stepping away can be hard; people with a history of anger problems almost never step away from situations that triggered their anger. Anger management programs are for people with persistent, uncontrollable anger and are designed to deal with very strong emotions in a healthy way. One of the best-known methods taught in any anger management program is the time-out strategy. Literally it means removing yourself from an adverse situation for a short period of time, usually an hour or so. What you are doing is finding personal space to analyze the source of your feelings; for example, irritation, anxiety or resentment. Personal space is useful when you need to cool off and gives you an opportunity to better cope with a bad situation.

Think about how time away from a negative situation can help give perspective and more beneficial coping strategies. With time away you are in a better position to learn constructive ways to lessen bad feelings and hopefully resolve the problem. Time out using comfortable personal space is about grounding yourself, reflecting and de-escalating. Of course, you need not distance yourself forever. Once you have calmed down and feel it is safe and useful to reconnect or move on, then distancing from other people is no longer needed.

WHEN TO ENLIST HELP

A self-help book like this one gives solid advice and tips on how you can better your living conditions, and it tells you how you can improve your mood and live a good life. There are several tools and skills offered and you can see for yourself how well they work for you. Try new strategies right away and examine the positive effects quickly. You need not depend on a therapist, friend or doctor to guide you towards self-improvement.

Do know, however, that self-help books only work well when you have good focus and when you can follow the information and benefit from good advice. If you suffer from severe anxiety, intolerable distress or chronic depression, the ability to concentrate and benefit from tips and strategies may be impaired. Feeling immobile and living with low energy levels and fatigue might deter you from using the strategies presented in this book. In this case, consider enlisting the aid of a mental health professional. Reading a book like this may be helpful but possibly not enough to take you to a better place.

Decide whether the challenges in your life are so great they will block you from the healing journey of working on yourself, by yourself. Keep the following points in mind as you decide whether it is worth getting help.

Enlist help if: you have a diagnosed psychiatric disorder not currently being treated. More than likely the symptoms demand immediate attention by a general practitioner (GP), psychiatrist or another mental health specialist. Psychotropic medication prescribed by a GP may be necessary to minimize distress, remove dark thoughts and get rid of other symptoms. You may need a medication review.

Enlist help if: you suspect you have a serious mental health issue. This should be assessed by a medical practitioner or a certified psychologist who can make a diagnosis if need be and follow through with a treatment plan.

Enlist help if: you feel compelled to disclose a painful experience or uncontrollable thoughts. A therapist is trained to listen non-judgementally and validate your experience. A therapist can advise when symptoms interfere with proper functioning and need immediate attention.

Keep an open mind. Who is the best person to bring you closer to emotional health and optimal functioning? Perhaps it is you with the aid of this guide, or perhaps it is a support person, coach, psychologist or counselor who can nudge you in a positive direction. A psychiatrist or GP can prescribe medications and make proper referrals. Getting professional help makes the most sense if you are finding it hard – bordering on impossible – to undertake the most basic functions of keeping yourself and loved ones safe and growing well. That said, this book will be handy whenever you are ready.

SUMMARY

Some solitude is helpful and should be initiated by you, no one else. Spending time understanding who you are and who you want to be will be gratifying. Embracing alone time most certainly does not equate with being depressed and withdrawn and it does not mean you will be distant, especially when you wish to be emotionally and physically close to other people and when togetherness is wanted by all parties.

If I am not mistaken, it should not be too difficult finding a special place for thinking and problem solving. After all, at one time in your life you occupied the same old surroundings due to a long-standing pandemic. At one time you might have tried figuring out whether household objects, both practical items and furniture pieces, were useful as you did more and more jobs from home. Perhaps you went all out and changed the décor and furnishings to brighten your pad. These examples point to enhancing your current personal space as a way of bringing your life to a better place.

There is a valuable lesson stemming from a persistent pandemic and quarantine: you know you are capable of thriving during extraordinary times. The pandemic forced you to hurriedly adapt to change and to carry on duties without much outside stimulation. Now you can better appreciate the difference between strict distancing or lockdown (a bad thing to live through) and voluntary solitude and repose (a good thing to work towards). Next we will be looking at ways you can use personal space and strategies to do many things, and I would like to emphasize that from here onwards the book delves into voluntary distancing and self-discovery across many areas of life.

Practice. Practice. Practice.

PART II

PRACTICE

There are times in life when it is helpful to embrace solitude and make a concerted effort to practice private thinking and reflection. Think of your health, which is vital to growth and existence into old age. Your health and safety are essential also to the development and success of your significant others and network of friends, who you protect and keep an eye on one way or another. When you practice cultivating personal space you do wonders to enhance your physical and emotional health and overall wellness. Let's go over how you will accomplish positive change in Part II.

In Part II, chapters 4 through 11 ask you to practice finding personal space for various purposes. In Chapter 4 you will learn how to boost your present-day level of physical activity. In Chapter 5 you will learn why it is good to have proper body posture. You will come to see that you – at your will and on your own – need not rely on public facilities, social groups or friends to stay energized and focused. That is to say, you can embark on active living fairly easily in the comfort of your home or neighborhood – a familiar place. As far as exercising good posture, which leads to self-control and confidence not to mention being crucial for body health and safety, the first step is to use some private time to be conscientious about your body position in different settings, social and otherwise.

In chapters 6 and 7 the take-home message is that you are better off dropping old, unhelpful behaviors and substituting them with refreshing and rewarding behaviors that give meaning and purpose. Chapter 6 introduces the concept of *introspection*: making good use of quiet time to look within yourself and consciously observe your thoughts and feelings. Only in solitude can you fully explore inner strengths and areas of need and make realistic or attainable goals for yourself. In this chapter you will also see the value of crafting and developing leisure skills. Creative skilled work, something you can perform solo, will give you the chance to express intense, maybe even painful, emotions using a positive outlet rather than keeping them bottled up in an unhealthy way.

Recall my important message from the introduction: when you embrace personal space it can set your mind to rest point while opening the door to positive outcomes. The mind is intelligent yet oftentimes wrestles with ruminating or dark thoughts. Therefore, some solitude is necessary when you must think clearly about how to manage a problem that gets in the way of happy living. In Chapter 7 you will monitor how you have been doing things day by day, which chores tend to bring you down and what kinds of enjoyable tasks you wish to add to your routine. A change in daily actions is important when you must get rid of depressed affect, deal with chronic depression or tackle burnout. Try crafts and leisure activities that are trending to dramatically shift your mood from sadness to happiness. Remember that you need not depend on other people to change your mood for the better, that you need only rely on yourself and your personal interests and strengths.

Naturally life has its ups and downs; it is incredibly hard to imagine adding fun things to the calendar when you are feeling stressed or overwhelmed. Anxiety and stress are the most common ailments affecting most of us today, which is not surprising considering how chaotic life gets for the average worker in the workforce, for the average caregiver and partner and for the average young person trying to make the right choices for a successful future. This is why it is important to turn to chapters 8 and 9 for simple-to-use exercises that can bring calm and peace.

In Chapter 8 you will look within and attend to your body's senses and their effects, something we generally tend not to do because of an otherwise autopilot mode of thinking and behaving. You will also be shown how to practice daily meditation. Meditation is a common strategy and one that is easy to adopt, especially with some practice. Additional mindfulness approaches are covered in Chapter 9, including crafting a gratitude letter and undertaking the happiness exercise regularly. Both strategies involve taking time to mentally examine your innermost thoughts and evaluate your feelings and then journaling them. For any form of mindfulness strategy you really need to find quiet space in order to properly attend to your present state of mind and keep you centered on the here and now. You can't be mindful without having some solitude and quiet.

I would be remiss if I did not share with you easy-to-do distraction methods to ward off worries and distress. Various distraction techniques are covered in Chapter 10, and in Chapter 11 I have you pick up a special trick for eliminating anxiety for the long haul. It involves riding out anxiety rather than constantly distracting yourself from it. You will learn how to face physiological anxiety head on and understand why uncomfortable internal sensations are there in the first place, something you can only truly grasp in the comfort of your personal space.

In chapters 4 through 11 I ask you to keep an open mind about various skills and self-soothing strategies to improve your physical and mental health and your satisfaction with life – all on your own. There are multiple ways for you to bring about positive change in Part II, so be prepared to practice cultivating personal space to live a happier and fulfilled life.

ACTIVATE
YOUR
BODY

The body achieves what the mind believes.

– AMERICAN SELF-HELP AUTHOR NAPOLEON HILL

recently came across a question and answer forum on Quora regarding what users liked about going to the gym. People like being thinner, stronger and toned. Improving physique is a common reason, but not the sole reason. For one guy it was peer pressure that got him to swallow an expensive premium membership. His buddies were working out any chance they got, and he simply wanted to fit in and follow the crowd. Another user admitted he went to the fitness center because his girlfriend made him join; evidently the girlfriend wanted company and valued her partner's moral support. A nursing student wrote a thoughtful reply about what the gym meant to her: "The gym is a safe place for me to gather my thoughts and be the best person I can be." I liked this reason the best.

TURNING PERSONAL SPACE INTO A PERSONAL GYM

There are several reasons why devoted patrons visit the local gym. Maintaining good body weight and developing muscle strength were the most common posts I saw on Quora, but suppose the gym facility was unavailable for some reason and left faithful users stumped about how to get fit. Forgive any unintentional stereotyping here; in no way am I implying that gym rats or fitness fanatics are unintelligent and can't easily solve this dilemma. Let me clarify by saying that anyone can be super motivated to get on top form but then never end up following through with fitness because they don't know where to begin.

Say the gym changed business hours, making it more or less inconvenient to drop in, or what if the center closed down permanently? The thought of not having a gym available for regular exercise is not as obscure as it sounds. In pandemic life, the need to halt public services and other venues temporarily became a reality and lockdown measures reduced large groups of people gathering in one small space. Evidently, COVID-19 passes along much more readily in tight quarters where fitness enthusiasts share metal and chrome equipment and sweat! However, the true sadness of it all was that some companies and public facilities did close their doors for good as they could not survive a huge loss in revenue.

If this was a barrier for you, how did you deal with it? Maybe you didn't bother to pursue good form, or maybe you tried something entirely different to stay in shape. This actually happened to a friend of mine. Louie was partial to weightlifting but had no weights of his own and no way of strengthening muscle tissue from home. In Louie's mind, all he wanted was to get inside the public gym facility to keep the fitness momentum going. What a shame, because the workout sounded great after his lazy weekend. Bear in mind that Louie is no lazy guy: he had been conditioning for weeks with the help of a fitness instructor and was very toned physically and feeling good. He then found out the gym was closed indefinitely and was disappointed. Again, let me repeat: Louie is not a lazy man nor a muscle head.

Most of us would feel unsure, maybe confused, if we were abruptly told to stop doing things that were once routine, predictable and welcomed. In a situation like that, suddenly we might find ourselves undecided about how to get back to our schedule or routine. I suspect this is what happened to Louie. As challenging as it appears, he didn't need to lose control of the situation. Instead, he needed to rebuild his desired goals using three easy steps:

- Assess the specific problem being faced during challenging times.
- Agree to accept exceptional circumstances that are beyond personal control.
- Find some space and practical tips to meet personal needs and desired goals.

If you experienced a similar fate, whether it was fitness related or not, follow these steps and make positive change in your own life, but first let's resolve Louie's situation.

| STEP 1: ASSESS THE SPECIFIC PROBLEM BEING FACED DURING CHALLENGING TIMES. | Louie should verbalize the problem so he understands it objectively. The lockdown might have been the result of public health officials minimizing the spread of a virus, or maybe the exercise place went into foreclosure for some reason. Understanding what led to the problem or what caused it will make it easier for Louie to accept the circumstances and move on. |
| STEP 2: AGREE TO ACCEPT EXCEPTIONAL CIRCUMSTANCES THAT ARE BEYOND PERSONAL CONTROL. | Louie must accept that he has no access to the gym, no equipment and no use of a trainer. He should think about different ways he can eliminate or reduce body fat and build strength to maintain his desired goals. What he (or any person) chooses depends on personal fitness goals: is the goal to have more muscle or more energy? He needs to think about other ways he can achieve that. |

STEP 3: FIND SOME SPACE AND PRACTICAL TIPS TO MEET PERSONAL NEEDS AND DESIRED GOALS.

Louie should seek advice on how to re-establish his fitness goals. He could try fitness apps and YouTube channels to source other ways to build muscle mass and strength without using any equipment at all; for instance, by doing squat jumps, burpees, flutter kicks, push ups, pull ups and so forth. He could also try something different such as yoga, which is a reasonable substitute for building strength. Louie has many options.

Louie found for himself an interesting solution to the conundrum and ended up solving more than one issue. Cycling caught his interest because he had always wanted to condition his upper leg muscles and abdomen. It was spring, and Louie looked forward to spending time outdoors and thought it would be fun to ride his new bike and uncover trails in the neighborhood. Voilà! Louie swiftly jumped back on the fitness horse.

BOOSTING PHYSICAL EXERCISE AT HOME

Walking, jogging, aerobics and recreation sports are forms of physical exercise. Obviously, some are more vigorous than others, but either way you look at it exercise produces a stronger heart. Chemicals released from the brain during exercise bring several benefits to your body and brain: better sleep, less joint pain and reduced stress. And if that's not enough to convince you to exercise more often, note that these chemicals make it possible to fight physical disease. You will stay physically healthy with regular exercise.

Not only that, but it is a well-known fact that exercise does more than improve functioning of the physical body. Physical exercise improves mental health. Studies have shown that anxiety and depression are reported less when we remain physically active compared with when we are inactive or sedentary. All in all, exercise is good for both body health *and* emotional health.

The World Health Organization (WHO) recommends that people at every age should make time each day to exercise. Why the emphasis on doing more physical activity? So little physical effort is required to do anything these days, because in modern life we can buy awesome-looking motorized bicycles and toss away the old 10 speeds and mountain bikes. We can step and glide on conveniently placed escalators and elevators while avoiding stairwells at the medical building or department store. Most occupations in an industrialized era involve sit-down office work; there is no more standing on the line. Actually, it's quite hard these days to find jobs demanding heavy labor, and just about everyone owns a shiny graphite computer. Among other things, we rely on the PC for banking, making purchases, visiting doctors and booking appointments at the nail salon and groomer. By today's standards, why does anyone need to *run* errands anyway?

The chart on the next page lists the amount of physical activity per 24-hour day or per week recommended by WHO. It represents the time per day for school-aged children and the suggested time per day that adults should be engaged in moderate-intensity physical activity in order to maintain good health. Find the recommended amount of physical activity for your age group and choose moderate intensity or high-impact, vigorous-intensity activity.

AGE	Recommended amount of physical activity (per day or per week)*
NEWBORNS, 0–12 MONTHS	No restrictions. Avoid restraining infants in a car seat, stroller or high chair for more than one hour at a time.
1–4 YEARS	180 minutes in a 24-hour day in various types of physical activities at any intensity: low impact, moderate intensity, high impact or vigorous.
5–17 YEARS	60 minutes per day on average of moderate- to vigorous-intensity physical activity across the week.
18–64 YEARS	150–300 minutes of moderate-intensity physical activity per day or 75–150 minutes of vigorous-intensity physical activity per day.
65+	The same as for 18–64 year olds. To prevent falls and injury, add physical activities that promote balance, coordination and muscle strengthening.

* WHO, November 2022, https://www.who.int/news-room/fact-sheets/detail/physical-activity

You can see that adults require more active periods compared with growing children. Adults have more sedentary behaviors than kids, who are ridiculously full of bounce. Sitting for long hours writing this manuscript using my laptop keyboard and a voice recorder is a case in point. It does not help that adults have a slower metabolism rate compared with children; the chemicals in body cells take longer in adults to convert calories into expendable energy. Therefore, as we age we must be purposeful in boosting physical activity.

> **Think wilfully about building physical activity into everyday life.**

Do you have endurance and don't mind working up a sweat? CrossFit, which is number one when it comes to vigorous activity, has movements for cardio and strength (squats, sit-ups, side kicks, heel touches, burpies) that are all at high intensity. Let me tell you about a former client of mine, 38-year-old Henry, who started a CrossFit class to try something invigorating. You may have heard that CrossFit is trending, and Henry was eager to be a part of this community so he gave it a try. However, he went to one class only before the pandemic forced the club to close its doors. That's the bad news; now for the good news: CrossFit can be done practically anywhere. Henry discovered that CrossFit can be done online using video instruction and a guide. No special equipment is needed other than a comfortable mat and a rope and some weights. Once Henry managed to collect the materials he kept up with the exercise from the comfort of his home.

There were three steps that made it possible for Henry to make positive changes:

- He learned that his much-desired CrossFit group class was canceled on account of the spike in Covid cases and that there was an immediate need for gym users to socially isolate.
- He realized they could not continue with group classes, at least not in the foreseeable future. It was disappointing to not be a part of a social community and participate in vigorous exercise.
- He researched CrossFit exercise online and happily discovered he could easily participate from home with minimal exercise equipment.

Not everyone's physique can handle the demands of a CrossFit drill. For full disclosure, the 20-minute aerobics workout on VHS that began for me as a fad in the 1990s also ended for me in the 1990s: it was just too much vigor for me. Even so, I suggest building some fitness into daily life. Be sensible and get a physician's stamp of approval if you have an existing heart condition, have had surgery recently or if you have a history of chronic medical problems.

My own preference for physical activity is power or speed walking, as walking comes naturally and is not taxing on body joints. Anyone who knows how to walk can do it regardless of their body strength, and just 10 minutes of brisk walking will promote alertness and a positive mood.

Will you be adding physical activity into your daily routine? Give power walking a try just for one week. Below are five tips to make a daily walking exercise easy to do and fun.

1. DECIDE THE LOCATION OF YOUR WALK	Find a location for walking that is conducive to daily practice. If you own a treadmill, step away from chores and retreat to your happy place. If you prefer landscapes and the natural movement of flora and fauna then walk around the block, weather permitting. By the way, being immersed in nature amid trees, sky and grass alters your brain waves and relaxes your body. It is also a scientific fact that people who spend more time in green space report being happier compared with those who spend more time indoors.
2. TAKE 30–50 MINUTES EACH DAY FOR A SPEED WALK	Use a moderate or fast pace rather than a leisurely stroll. Begin with a 10-minute duration of moderate-intensity walking then bump it up to 15–20 minutes per day. Eventually increase it to 30, 40 and then 50 minutes of speed walking per day.

3. ALTERNATE BETWEEN A LIGHT JOG AND BRISK WALKING	If you are up for the challenge, toggle between 60 seconds of a light jog and 5 minutes of brisk walking, a method encouraged by doctors because of the benefits to the cardiovascular system. Check with your GP that exercise will be all right for your body.
4. WALK WITH A BUDDY	Solitude during your walk is not a bad thing as it gives you ample time to think carefully about things, but if you can coordinate it then walk with a partner or your child. Walking with a buddy opens the door to good conversation and is an easy way to stay connected. Walking with your dog is obviously good for your pet's health and attitude, just as walking is beneficial to you.
5. ENLIST A COACH TO HELP WITH YOUR FITNESS GOALS	Use a coach or guide to help with your fitness goals. Doing any form of exercise from home usually means you cannot profit from a gym instructor, but note that there are many digital apps and YouTube videos available to support you with your fitness goals.

CHAPTER 5

STAND
TALL

*When it comes to posture, your
mother knew best. Her reminders to
stop slouching were good advice.*

– MAYO FOUNDATION FOR MEDICAL
EDUCATION AND RESEARCH

magine standing with your feet planted firmly in your personal space. Is your head looking down and is your body hunched over as though you were avoiding eye gaze, or are you the type who stands confidently tall waiting for a delightful conversation to begin? Your body posture is a signal that says a lot about your confidence level and general style.

How you position your body also says something about your habits. My mother perpetually spoke an annoying three words when I was a kid: "Sit up straight." She had a knack of tending to my body carriage over and over again whenever I least expected it: when I casually walked to the fridge to fetch a snack, while chilling in front of the tube or when my family hosted a big Italian-style dinner with brow-raising aunts and uncles. The seriousness of the parental tone of voice was convincing enough to pull me upright and stiff ... that is, until mia mama got distracted and turned away, when I regressed slowly downward to the favored slump. You see, my caring mother was fretful that as a growing child I would eventually take on a permanent slouch or some other anomaly. Paolina was right about many things, but she was wrong about that – thankfully.

However, the wise woman was on to something: the value of having good posture. Poor body position contributes to certain hazards that we as mature adults ought not to ignore. Ongoing bad posture can lead to fatigue, falls, tension headaches, back pain and breathing problems. Reflect on your own typical posture:

- Do I slouch when eating a meal or reading a magazine?
- Am I bending forward towards the laptop screen?
- Is my neck stooped down when scrolling through texts?
- Is there chronic pain in my joints, back and neck?

There is physical stress on the body whenever you lean in a slouched position. In a leaning forward position, all of the weight shifts head first and there is a good chance you will lose your balance and topple. If you need a visual, try to picture the way a one-year-old baby eagerly learning how to take footsteps for the first time walks, or think of the forward-leaning gait of a drunken sailor stumbling along the marina docks. Falling over is less likely to happen when your body is aligned vertically with the floor, because when your body is upright your weight is equally distributed over both feet and that makes it virtually impossible to trip up (unless you truly are inebriated). Therefore, standing tall is the best way to maintain balance and prevent falls and other injuries.

Sitting or standing straight puts less stress on your lower back and less tension in your neck. Also, there is less compression of the internal organs when your body is stretched. With more internal space there is better circulation of blood and oxygen, especially in the nerves of your back and legs. Think of other things that happen inside when you stand erect: your diaphragm contracts better, your lungs have more space to enlarge and breathing becomes deeper. The health benefits of standing straight include:

- deeper breathing and the circulation of oxygen
- better digestion of food
- reduced tension in your neck muscles and lower back
- fewer headaches.

Visualize what you should look like during a meditation exercise: cross-legged on a flat surface with your torso elongated in a full vertical position. Ever wonder why this body position, known as the lotus position, is best for a calming practice? In meditation the lotus position is appropriate because it helps keep your mind focused while at the same time relaxing your body. Have you ever seen anyone meditate leaning against a headboard? How about on a beanbag chair? Laid-back positions are discouraged during meditation poses, as sitting slouched does not match up well with keeping your mind on the present and eliciting calm and peace.

Researchers who study embodied cognition maintain that how you position your body affects how you think about things and how you act on the environment. As an illustration, envision your body loosely seated on a sofa in a relaxed, laid-back position then imagine chatting happily with a buddy while together you casually watch a ball game. In embodied cognition it is argued that the body pose – in this case the slouched stance – gives important information to your brain. It tells your brain that you are thoroughly relaxed and easy-going and enjoying the game. Even more, it informs your brain that you are agreeable. The slouched pose suggests that you are less rigid in your opinions and more open to new ideas and suggestions. Bottom line: *how you sit tells your brain how you think.*

We are halfway there. Next, consider the relationship between your laid-back body posture and your actions. In a laid-back stance you feel more at ease and secure, so much so that you casually agree with what your friend is suggesting or proposing. In other words, while deep in the game you give no second thought, quickly nod your head and smile when your friend offers up another round of beer and refills the bowl of potato chips.

Slouching pose → *(leads to) Laid back / relaxed opinions* → *Consuming more chips and beer*

The idea that body position and mind are linked is supported by research in the lab. Belgian Jiska Eelen and American Aparna Labroo did a clever experiment, inviting participants to perform a mental task while seated either in a relaxed position or perfectly upright. Every volunteer who participated in that experiment was offered grapes as a snack during the task. Okay, let me divulge that the fruit was not offered up just to be nice. Participants were unaware of this, but the researchers cared less about the mental exercise itself and more about how many grapes each person ended up eating. (By the way, investigators of human behavior very much enjoy using deception tactics to get a peek at honest responses.)

The more you consume the more you indulge, right? The researchers next recorded how many grapes were left over after the session finished and, as predicted by the experimenters, people sitting in the relaxed position left fewer grapes on the table. In other words, the so-called slouchers ate more grapes. Being in a relaxed state, they casually snacked quite a bit while doing the mental task. In contrast, the research participants who sat tall did the opposite to the slouchers: those in a perfectly upright pose snacked on fewer grapes while performing the mental exercise.

This study makes an important point about how people tend to do things in everyday life. Let's start with informal settings: in more relaxed settings it is acceptable to be carefree and unaware of how much you are enjoying things, and pamper yourself when the opportunity arises. Put another way, sometimes it really does not matter how many potato chips you consume while casually enjoying the ball game on TV. Eating high-fat foods is not super healthy for you, but we all know it happens from time to time to keep up the fun and camaraderie.

Now let's consider more formal settings. Good posture primes people to be prudent in situations that call for more formality and playing it safe; that is, good posture is better for you during proper family events such as having a holiday dinner with relatives. Good posture is important in work settings such as when you are introducing yourself to an employer in a job interview. Sitting up tall lets others around you know that you are attentive, thoughtful and respectful.

Are you now beginning to see the value of good posture?

Good posture has other benefits, with research indicating that it makes you think about events in a more positive way while bad posture makes you think about situations more negatively. In one psychology study participants did some really hard math questions while seated either perfectly straight or slouched. For those particpants who were sitting tall their reactions to difficult math exercises were found to be more positive: they felt less helpless with challenging questions, were confident answering harder questions and were proud of their performance. On the other hand, participants who were slouched had a big disadvantage in that they had more trouble with the math exercises, as being in a relaxed frame of reference actually made the mental task a lot harder for them. Honestly, it is amazing to know that how a person holds their body posture affects how difficult to do they find a task!

The take-home messages from research studies on posture are these:

- Slouching produces less self-control and less confidence.
- Sitting upright does the opposite: it gives you self-control.
- Good posture improves confidence and positivity.

In light of the differences between good and bad posture, keep an eye on your body position and movements next time you are strolling along the street, seated at a dinner party, having a conversation with a friend or meeting with the boss. Start to pay attention to the position of your body in different settings. Proper posture is not necessary for everything you do, but sometimes it helps to stay tall.

CHAPTER
—
6

BE KIND
TO YOUR SOUL

Depression doesn't take away your talents
— it just makes them harder to find.

– ENTERTAINER LADY GAGA

Most of my clients present with anxiety, with depression and perfectionism being close seconds when it comes to mental health concerns. Lately I have noticed a spike in major depression, the sharp rise in sadness, irritability, lack of energy and poor concentration corresponding with a long-standing pandemic. More people now say they are unmotivated and disinterested in doing fun activities that at one time they enjoyed doing. This reduced interest is what psychologists call "anhedonia" and is the hallmark of mood disorders such as major depressive disorder and dysthymia, or chronic depression.

CASE STUDY: SELENA

Seventeen-year-old Selena came to my practice with her mother, who was concerned because Selena had lost the desire to be around family. She adamantly refused to eat meals and go to school, which was surprising to everyone who knew her because Selena was a bright teenager who cared about doing well in school. As a competitive swimmer she was the type of person who had always promoted healthy eating and living.

In our private session Selena admitted that she felt anxious around her peers, worrying that she might do or say something embarrassing. As it turned out, she had been bullied by a classmate in elementary school and lost many friends. Over the years she developed poor body image, saying that she was overweight. She felt unworthy. Selena stopped eating, partly because she wanted to lose weight but also because she had lost her appetite. It is noteworthy that she felt sad all the time, was no longer energetic and did not find life worth living. Her mood had been persistently low over the preceding few weeks. She presented with a normal body mass index for her height and age, but it was clear she was at risk of developing an eating disorder. Importantly, I diagnosed Selena with major depressive disorder.

In Selena's case there were self-esteem issues going back to her childhood that resurfaced once she started high school. Her high school friends were pretty and popular but in no way kind towards Selena. She was constantly judged for the clothing she wore, her hairstyle and body shape.

It makes you wonder why she stayed friendly with this peer group; it could be that Selena internalized negative comments, believing she was inferior to the popular girls. I need not remind you that adolescent beings can be very hard on each other. An important note I gathered from my assessment was that Selena did not have one single friend she felt she could trust, that there was no one she bonded with. One of the things we worked on was building a network of friends she could count on. We also worked on her negative self-perceptions and on rebuilding self-worth.

There are many reasons why people feel depressed. Living alone and spending too much time in the absence of fun activities and company is depressing when social gatherings are something you desire, plus I have already mentioned the ill effects of quarantine on social life. Depression can occur when you've experienced a significant life event such as the death of a loved one or being separated from a spouse or child. Geography plays a role as well: if you live in a cold climate you might fall prey to seasonal depression. A collection of depressive symptoms – low energy, sadness, oversleeping, overeating and irritability – co-exist with long harsh winters, staying cooped up at home and waiting for the cold weather and gray skies to finally let up.

Depression is not uncommon in present-day society, affecting 10 percent of adults living in America and not less than 5 percent of individuals globally. According to the World Health Organization, depression alone can be worse for your health compared with chronic diseases such as diabetes, angina, asthma and arthritis. Consider these questions:

- How do you spend free time these days?
- What forms of entertainment do you enjoy?
- Are you missing the drive to do something exciting?
- Are you feeling sad?

Did you answer "Yes" to any of these questions? Depression does not usually go away with one big change. Typically, it takes several baby steps to change how we view the world and how we perceive ourselves.

One way to chip away at a depressed mood is to find things in life that give you purpose, to look for something that gives you meaning. The human adult mind is intelligent, and common thinking would suggest that exercising this smart brain and looking at the world with a positive lens require special materials and a ton of effort – but it does not. Even in the absence of people, sociable events or sunny skies you can do wonderful things for the soul, but you will need personal space and a plan.

INTROSPECTION

As you breathe right now, another person takes their last. So stop complaining, and learn to live your life with what you have.

– ANONYMOUS

No one is perfect. Introspection involves looking within and exploring thoughts and feelings, and it means paying attention to accomplishments you have made and evaluating challenges you have faced. Your introspection provides a candid look at your personal strengths and areas of need, an important first step in determining how you might compensate for limitations or overcome weaknesses. Of course, sometimes you have to just live with what you've got.

Consider some major events from your past. How have you managed difficult situations before? Might you do certain things differently today if you had the chance? Because of your growth and where you are today, previous situations are generally viewed with a different lens. Today you have a perspective on things that you did not have in the past when caught up in issues, but it is best not to dwell on old decisions. Learn from past mistakes, work towards new goals and find ways to achieve those goals.

I asked friends to share some of their desired goals at the current point in their lives. I asked each person to be introspective, meaning I told each person to focus on personal strengths, limitations and what they felt they could (or possibly could not) change in their lives. Comments were made by adolescents, university students, working adults, married couples, divorced couples and seniors, who spoke about education, occupation, relationships and anything else that came to mind. Some interesting themes evolved from the poll.

Finding my passion

- I wish for a new job with more responsibility.
- I want to make a difference and volunteer at a youth crisis center.
- I want to learn how to assist first responders with post-traumatic stress disorder so I will register for a continuing education course on trauma.
- I'm retired and still haven't found something that makes me feel useful. I want to find a cause and pursue it.

I care more about quality of life and less about money

- I quit a decent-paying job to start up a business venture; despite the financial risk the change was thrilling.
- I asked the boss to cut back my hours to make time for my elderly parents.
- I will work fewer hours at my part-time job to study more for better grades.

Needing life skills to thrive

- I could learn how to cook, drive a car and manage money better.
- I should walk the family dog and tidy up my room without being told.
- I value my health so I will run a marathon a few years from now.
- Even though I am shy I want to meet people.

I love my family

- We hope to see our grandkids every other week when they visit their dad.
- My wife agreed to couples counseling to forgive and help get trust back.
- I rarely see my nine-year-old twins after the divorce; I want to be there for my children.
- My husband and I are planning a weekend getaway to rekindle the romance.

Personal growth is important to me

- I've always wanted to learn a new language.
- It is important to accept diversity in the world.
- It'd be nice to travel abroad.
- I'm thinking about trying a challenging sport such as kickboxing or snowboarding.
- My therapist says I should develop self-compassion.

This is a healthy list of action items to make positive change and live a happier life. Do any of these aspirations resonate with you? Can you think of goals that inspire you?

SKILL DEVELOPING AND SELF-EXPRESSION

Introspection does not require you to rely on friends, experts or anyone for that matter to make you feel better about yourself. The same is true when you develop a skill or craft. The goal in skill developing is to change what is important in your life and feel good about your accomplishments. Sometimes these are small accomplishments, but that doesn't matter.

I rediscovered the fun of knitting after 40 or so years. I started thinking about it during the long pandemic when I was utterly bored to tears, but for the life of me I couldn't remember how to get started. As sales associates darted past me at the local craft store, I quickly learned that I would not be in line for assistance any time soon; perhaps my fellow shoppers had the same idea during lockdown and were also in a frenzy. I had little time to wait and the best option was to go home and do some research. Without anyone around to help, I did an online search for videos that gave instructions for making the knitting project a reality. I remembered to obey the three steps from Chapter 4 and knew I needed to follow through with my knitting goal.

1. I ASSESSED THE SPECIFIC PROBLEM BEING FACED DURING CHALLENGING TIMES (IN THIS CASE THE PANDEMIC)	I was getting bored watching TV and thought it would be cool to try knitting again. It was winter and I wanted to learn how to make a wool blanket.
2. I ACCEPTED EXCEPTIONAL CIRCUMSTANCES THAT WERE BEYOND MY PERSONAL CONTROL	I didn't have time to wait at the busy craft store for expert advice. If I wanted to start soon, I would figure out another way to learn how to knit.
3. I FOUND SOME SPACE AND PRACTICAL TIPS TO MEET MY PERSONAL NEEDS AND DESIRED GOALS	I did a google search to relearn how to knit and looked up YouTube videos on basic knitting stitches. I bought materials for a chunky wool blanket and practiced until I was able to do the stitches correctly.

These days it is fashionable to make painted rocks, scrapbooks and candles, among many other crafts. It can give you a feeling of pride in the same way that wood-burning art did for Shanice, a 40-year-old librarian.

Wood burning, or pyrography, is freehand drawing on pieces of wood using a heated poker. Shanice made some interesting pieces such as welcome signboards for the porch, stenciled images of much-adored family pets and personalized key chains. Friends have commissioned Shanice to produce memorials and custom house signs, and she appreciates their confidence in her. I asked her to tell me why she chose wood burning as a pastime, and she replied that it kept her mind busy but most of all she felt proud.

A craft or hobby is not just a pastime.
What you create with your hands gives
you a sense of accomplishment.

I must say I was both amazed by such a positive outlook and kind of shocked when Shanice said that wood-burning art changed her mood for the better. Why was I surprised? You see, Shanice is a long-standing client of mine who came to me two years prior with major depression. For the previous two years she had been feeling run down, unmotivated and dreading going to her workplace, a large, busy public library. In the past she had made little time for exercise, socializing and leisure activities because she was always tired and unhappy, and to make it worse three years ago Shanice was disabled with thoughts of suicide. The depression got in the way of living – but that was before.

I must say I was relieved that Shanice found value in wood-burning art. She had a dazzling look in her eyes when she spoke about this special craft. Because of its positive effects, our treatment plan included the art of wood burning as an ongoing hobby. Shanice does this in a spare room at home and sometimes on her balcony. In future therapy sessions she and I will explore other activities to boost her newfound energy and sense of self-worth.

Going back to my knitting project, I ended up learning a simple but cute knit and purl stitch pattern, then I made a gorgeous cream-colored chunky blanket that drapes lovingly over the living room sofa. You could say that I too am feeling proud and confident.

Psychiatrists and married co-authors Drs Carrie and Alton Barron suggest that creative skilled work such as knitting and wood burning has positive health benefits beyond feelings of joy and satisfaction. Crafting is a form of self-expression. They argue that through a creative outlet our minds express ruminating thoughts and complex emotions that we generally try to bury inside: underlying tension, anger, self-loathing and worthlessness. I believe self-expression in wood-burning art is a big reason why Shanice was able to overcome depression.

> **Do you ever bottle up intense emotions?**
> **Did burying your feelings end**
> **up making you feel worse?**

If you don't express negative emotions via words or by doing something with your hands then bad feelings and thoughts fester. They build up over time, then the load becomes too much and results in irritability or even explosiveness. At other times it leads to anger turned inward, better known as depression. The famous theorist and psychoanalyst Sigmund Freud argued that repressed or bottled-up emotions, many of which stemmed from childhood experiences and trauma, will come back to haunt us at some point. According to Freud: "Unexpressed emotions will never die. They are buried alive and will come forth later in uglier ways."

Now you know there is much value in expressing your emotions via a craft or hobby because it is good for your emotional health. Try crafting for the love of a pastime and relaxation and for your self-esteem. If creative work is new to you I suggest a google search and YouTube videos for ideas. In the meantime, glance over these popular activities for some ideas.

Therapeutic coloring	Crocheting	Kinetic sand sculpting	Sketching	Journal writing
Making sachets and bath bombs	Using fabric dye	Aboriginal-style dot painting	Organic gardening	Watercolor painting
Hand embroidery	Pottery	Macramé wall hangings	Loom knitting	Photography
Pressed-flower candle making	Creating mandalas	Poetry writing	Culinary classes	Learning how to play a musical instrument

ACTIVATE
FUN
BEHAVIORS

Live as if you were to die tomorrow;
learn as if you were to live forever.

– POLITICAL ETHICIST MAHATMA GANDHI

Have you ever felt sad but you weren't sure why? Maybe you were feeling okay one minute and then your mood suddenly dropped, but sometimes it is not obvious what causes drastic mood changes. A change in emotions can happen fast because of a fleeting or automatic thought, and oftentimes it is hard to know what actions to take to eliminate bad feelings.

"Behavioral activation," a fancy name for a simple yet useful skill to get rid of depressed feelings, originated from cognitive behavioral therapy. I have used it to help clients notice the connection between sensations or feelings and their behaviors. In behavioral activation all you do is monitor the events or tasks you undertake from morning to bedtime, then you analyze your daily activities one by one. Which activities were fun to do? Which tasks tended to bring on sadness, exhaustion and low mood? The goal of activity monitoring is to identify any unhelpful activities and reduce or eliminate them where possible. In their place, the third step has you finding new activities that improve your mood.

Think about the types of activities you did today. Which ones were fun and gave you a smile? What proportion of your day involved these pleasant activities? Could you use more pleasant times to improve your mood?

Behavioral activation is of value if you find yourself saying these things:

- I don't have much energy; I'm tired all the time.
- The things I do don't give me meaning.
- I think I know why I'm feeling sad but I'm not 100 percent sure.
- I don't like my routine.

Behavioral activation is easy to implement. First, find some private space to jot down the kinds of tasks, chores and activities you accomplish over the course of the day from the moment you rise until bedtime. Sometimes it is easier to simply list events in their order of occurrence each day, such as eating breakfast, taking the train to work, meeting a friend for lunch, going to the gym after work and so on. Think about the connections between those activities and your feelings. Do the tasks make you feel good, or are they making you feel irritated or sad? Use a pen and paper to make connections between your behaviors and your emotions. Once you figure out what kinds of activities make you feel good or better, make a commitment to build new, positive tasks into your daily routine. Follow these five steps in your behavioral activation.

1. Find private space and a paper and pencil or a word processor that is handy for creating lists.

2. Monitor your activities from morning to evening. Record all of your activities every single day for one week. You can use the template below and choose your own start and end times.

TIME	MY ACTIVITY TODAY
7.00 AM	
8.00 AM	
9.00 AM	
10.00 AM	
11.00 AM	
12.00 PM	
1.00 PM	
2.00 PM	
3.00 PM	
4.00 PM	
5.00 PM	
6.00 PM	
7.00 PM	
8.00 PM	
9.00 PM	
10.00 PM	

3. At the end of one week make two lists: one for the activities that were fun to do and one for the activities that gave you bad feelings such as a low mood, anxiety, irritability or boredom.

ACTIVITES THAT MADE ME HAPPY

1. _____

2. _____

3. _____

ACTIVITES THAT MADE ME SAD AND ANXIOUS

1. _____

2. _____

3. _____

4. Find new activities you think will make you feel happier and satisfied via research on the internet or discussing your goals with someone who knows you well and can offer suggestions.

5. Replace unhelpful activities with new activities. Monitor your emotions over time and check for a positive change in your mood.

Let's take a look at how behavioral activation helped two people, Rai and Maria. By coincidence, both individuals in these scenarios are middle-aged adults. I'd like to point out that age itself is not a critical factor in whether behavioral activation will work or not, as the key to changing mood for the better is a willingness to give behavioral activation a try. Of course, you should be prepared to follow through with some homework. Honestly, the homework assignment is not time-consuming and certainly not hard to do, but I do appreciate the dilemma of adding any new assignments to an existing full workload no matter how little time they take.

RAI

Rai, a 59-year-old bank employee, has anxiety and depression. He experiences fatigue and sadness and worries that his manager is dissatisfied with his performance as a loans officer. He believes that one day he will be terminated even though nothing has been said to him about poor work performance in the past. In his free time Rai spends weekend mornings in bed. When he is not sleeping he usually lounges on the sofa watching TV, and he rarely visits his adult children except on special occasions. He does not have leisure activities other than TV and hasn't been hanging around his old buddies for more than a year.

Behavioral activation can help Rai resolve his depression and anxiety. The first step is to ask him to monitor his activities every day for an entire week. Keep in mind his energy and motivation are at a low and his body is a little sluggish, common features of depression, and that because of this it was not surprising he had trouble completing the homework. He needed reminders. The good news is that Rai eventually completed the monitoring, and this was the list of activities he reported for the Friday of the week:

TIME	RAI'S ACTIVITY
7.00 AM	Woke up, made a pot of coffee, glanced over emails
8.00 AM 9.00 AM	Shaved, dressed for work, grabbed a coffee at the drive-through on the way to the bank
10.00 AM	Met with customers
12.00 PM	Quick lunch; video conference call with managers at head office
1.00 PM	Trained a new employee
3.00 PM	Took a coffee break with co-workers

3.30 PM	Completed paperwork and answered phone messages
6.00 PM	Went to granddaughter's birthday party
8.00 PM	Tuned in to Netflix programming
10.00 PM	Bedtime

Rai was asked to link each activity with how he was feeling, for which he needed to create two more lists: one for activities that made him feel good and the other list for activities that made him feel anxious or depressed. I should point out that Rai admitted he did not do the homework this time as he just didn't feel up to making lists after an exhausting week. That's okay: I could help him create the two lists but needed to remind him that the task was not very difficult or time consuming. This is what we came up with together:

ACTIVITIES THAT MADE RAI HAPPY (OR LESS DEPRESSED)	ACTIVITIES THAT MADE RAI SAD AND ANXIOUS
Hanging with friends	Desk work for long periods
Spending time with family	Watching TV
Drinking the first cup of coffee	Speaking with the manager

The third and final step for Rai involved making a commitment to change his daily routine. He was encouraged to drop unhelpful activities and replace them with new activities that would elevate his mood. Here are some positive suggestions for Rai:

♀ Rai was known to spend a lot of time working at his desk and gave himself few break periods away from work. He was advised to make more time each day for a sit-down lunch period away from work papers and tasks. Perhaps he could sit outside at the park for a bag lunch or have lunch in a restaurant or lunchroom. He may want to share the breaktime with others and ask co-workers to join him.

- ‚ Given the nature of his office work, Rai will make time for several body and mind breaks throughout the day to stretch his legs and clear his head.

- ‚ Rai feels better when spending time with friends and family, less so when he feels that he is being judged by his boss. Therefore, he agreed to reach out to friends and perhaps join them for a game of golf or darts at the local pub. He hadn't seen his kids for a while and was excited about inviting his son, daughter-in-law and grandchild for Sunday dinner.

- ‚ Rai will consider counselling for performance anxiety. Of course, he will want to confirm that he is overreacting rather than there being a real problem with his performance on the job. Therefore, he scheduled a meeting with his supervisor and asked for a review of his work performance.

- ‚ Rai consumes a lot of coffee, which can make him edgy and irritable. He realized he should cut back on caffeine and agreed to have just one favourite cup of java in the morning. He will replace coffee with refreshing fruit drinks, non-caffeinated iced tea and iced water.

MARIA

Maria is a middle-aged wife and the mother of two teenage boys. Lately she has been feeling sad, teary-eyed and tired. Her elderly mother-in-law moved into the family home last year, and since the move-in both Maria and her husband Joe have been burdened with caregiving and work. Maria misses not spending as much time as she would like with her sons and her husband because of their busy schedules, and she doesn't reach out to her sister either despite having had a close relationship in the past.

Here is how behavioral activation helped Maria. She began to monitor her daily activities, and it didn't take long for her to conclude that she does mundane chores every single day: washing clothes, vacuuming, cleaning bathrooms, making meals and driving the boys to baseball practice. Not to mention that Maria takes good care of her mother-in-law by dressing her, styling her hair, giving her medication and playing cards together. Maria coordinates tasks with the personal support worker (PSW) and sometimes they work as a team to bathe the elder. On occasion the PSW offers to drive the mother-in-law to doctors' appointments. Maria spends, at most, an hour in leisure per day, usually at the very end of a long day. Sometimes she spends free time talking to Joe while drinking tea at the kitchen table.

When it was time for Maria to create two lists she had no trouble identifying which tasks made her feel anxious, tired and unhappy. Some chores made her feel unmotivated and super tired, such as dressing and bathing her mother-in-law and driving her teenagers to various events. She came up with only one single activity that gave her pleasure: she liked late evenings when she and Joe put their feet up, talked about things and laughed together.

Next Maria identified new goals, building rest periods and leisure time into her busy schedule. She brainstormed new activities she would be willing to try such as bike riding with her sister, taking a bubble bath, reading a fantasy novel, swimming in the backyard pool with the family and making homemade soup and pasta. To make time for new activities she delegated household chores to family members: the boys agreed to load the dishwasher each evening, launder their clothes on Sunday and tidy up their bedroom once per week, while Joe agreed to drive his sons to school in the mornings on his way to work, take them to ball practice on Wednesdays and, on occasion, take his mother to her medical appointments. The PSW had her work hours increased to help with elder caregiving, which was something both Maria and Joe agreed would give them a lot more time to do things as a couple and as a family.

*** * ***

Do either of these two stories resonate with you? Both Rai and Maria had depression. Anyone can have low mood, but it happens a lot for people with a busy work schedule and long work days. Depressed affect and burnout can be a problem in caregivers who are overcome with responsibilities, concerns and a sense of obligation for the welfare of others. Perhaps you have a heavy workload, or children or an elderly parent to look after. Try out behavioral activation to boost your mood.

SUMMARY

You can depend less on the outside, social world and more on your own skills and personal interests to self-soothe, energize and have fun. In previous chapters we explored physical exercise, body posture, introspection and crafting, and in this chapter you saw that you can monitor your activities for each day, make lists and add interesting and fun activities into the weekly planner. Behavioral activation is a good fit for you if you are feeling low, are overwhelmed by a busy calendar and if activities that would ordinarily give pleasure and meaning are no longer doing that. Pleasant and rewarding activities have been missing and should be introduced into your life.

STAY
MINDFUL

*When you pay attention to boredom
it gets unbelievably interesting.*

– JON KABAT-ZINN, SCIENTIST AND CREATOR OF
MINDFULNESS-BASED STRESS REDUCTION

Looking back at the previous chapters, it appears that fitting activities and crafts into your planner is a good way to restore balance in your life. After all, who wouldn't want a dose of excitement and novelty to put an end to the boredom that comes with tedious chores? Why not welcome fun activities and a change of pace to overcome the stress and occasional burnout that comes with a busy lifestyle? A huge boost in arousal level that comes from speed walking, crafting, playing an instrument or reading a great novel is more than enough to get moving in the direction of positive change.

Sometimes, however, we profit less from over-stimulation and more from calm. Living in a fast-paced world means that stressors are plentiful. Almost half of the adult population in North America currently suffers from physical ailments and mental illness, problems that are caused or made worse by high levels of stress. Mental stress originates from the demands of work, managing finances and dealing with interpersonal relationships and losses. Because of the potential to be over-stressed, it is in your best interest to find private space and bring back a relaxed state of being; that is, to bring calm and peace.

How will you restore calm and peace in your life?

Mindfulness is a way of life that aims to bring you calm. It does not eliminate existing stressors but it does allow you to pay attention to what is happening so that you feel less shocked and devastated by those stressors. It puts negative situations into a healthy perspective so that you can move forward and enjoy what you have . . . today.

It is a lifestyle choice to commit each day to mindfulness, which is not one single technique but an assortment of approaches to get you more in tune with the workings of your mind and body. These approaches share the goal of eliminating automatic thinking while encouraging you to think and feel in the present. It means being deliberate in your actions and staying non-judgemental in the way you approach people and events.

Life is filled with ups and downs, and mindfulness is particularly helpful when dealing with a difficult situation and tackling trying times. The key is to recognize and deal with problems you are facing right now, not ignore issues or pretend they do not exist. Nor is it healthy to react harshly to life's events: accept them as they are and be willing to push through and thrive.

The two mindfulness exercises outlined below will bring calm and peace. Both should be done in a quiet space so you can more easily attend to your state of mind, and you should make sure your private space is free from outside forces, social events and other distractions.

EXERCISE 1:
TAKE IN THE FIVE SENSES

Vision, hearing, touch, smell and taste are senses that help you navigate the world in a meaningful and safe way. Because of their survival value, all five senses are present at birth and have been remarkably functional since the day you were born (although hearing and sight take many months to fully mature). All of this highlights their importance in everyday life.

The five human senses are critical for:

- driving a vehicle, talking to friends and colleagues
- doing coursework, performing job duties, caring for significant others
- enjoying a meal, listening to music, playing musical instruments
- walking, maintaining balance, avoiding obstacles and physical danger.

Most of us give little thought to how each of the senses do their job. Actually, we do think about it from time to time, usually when something out of the ordinary happens to reduce their effectiveness. I recall, with reluctance, a recent visit to my dentist that involved freezing of my lower gum and a lengthy tooth procedure. Afterward, I stopped at a nearby café for a coffee to take with me on my next stop to the office. After taking that first sip I distinctly remember not being able to feel the rim of the cup against my lips. I felt embarrassed drinking and nervous about spilling it down my chin. I also did not enjoy the bitter taste because my tongue was completely numb from the freezing.

Although not always on the radar, our senses consistently work to gather information from the environment and interpret it. Sensory cells, or receptors, send messages to our nervous system: our brain. Each of the five senses has its own special sensors and unique way of capturing information so it can be understood by our brains.

The table below shows what each of the senses picks up from the environment. Each sense picks up something different, yet they work together to help you act upon the environment. Without any senses at all you would have no idea about what was going on and would not be able to act on the world and function properly.

HUMAN SENSES	WHAT THEY PICK UP
VISION	Receptor cells in your brain and the back of your eyes (the retina) detect light, color, movement, patterns and objects.
HEARING	Hair cells in your eardrums move according to audio frequencies, giving the perception of loudness. Auditory cells located in your brain detect the location of a sound as well as speech sounds.
TASTE	Taste buds located on different areas of your tongue are sensitive to distinct chemicals in foods, allowing you to detect salty, sour, bitter and sweet.
SMELL	Hair follicles in your nostrils pick up chemicals released from air molecules. Smell also comes from your mouth: when food is in your mouth, odors travel up into the nostrils and give food its flavor.
TOUCH	Below your skin (the epidermis) are skin receptors of different shapes and sizes that respond to pressure, vibrations and pain.

I want you to fully connect with all five senses in a deliberate way via the three following sensory activities. My favorites are dining in the dark and watching a pot of water boil. The activities are courtesy of Alexis Grosofsky at Beloit College, Wisconsin, who teaches sensation and perception to students of psychology.

Sensory activity 1: dining in the dark. How much do you rely on the sense of sight while eating a meal? Try to change that to see the effects by doing yourself the pleasure of eating a meal without vision:

- Once seated at the table with your dinner plate before you and cutlery within reach, don a blindfold.
- Remain blindfolded throughout the meal. For your safety, remove the blindfold if you need to get up from the table for whatever reason.
- After your meal is over and you have removed the blindfold, evaluate this sensory experience. How did your food taste, and what do you like about dining this way?

My friend Barb has a daughter, Katie, who did her graduate studies overseas and called home one day quite excited about what she had been up to while living abroad. Katie said to her mum: "Did you know that some restaurants invite patrons to eat meals in a pitch-black dining room? I tried one with friends: it was awesome. It was a bit weird at first, but then we really liked the chef's dishes." By removing the sense of sight the other senses contributed to the eating experience in a unique way. By focusing not on what she saw but on what she tasted, smelled and felt, Katie found her meal to be tastier and more enjoyable.

Several restaurants around the world offer this special dining experience; if you have the inclination to, do a google search to discover dark restaurants near you. Dark dining is a good way to keep in touch with the present and appreciate what we have. What do food critics say when they try dark restaurants? What are the customers' reviews?

Sensory activity 2: a watched pot never boils. I don't have to tell you that watching things and waiting for something to happen can feel like an eternity, but we also know that watched pots do boil . . . eventually. In this activity you will watch a pot of water come to a boil, and you will be surprised to find that within a short period of time – 5 minutes or so – a lot happens:

- Select a small pot and add water.
- Heat the water to boiling on a stovetop; it takes approximately 5 minutes.
- Observe the cooking pot the entire time then note on paper all that you see, hear, feel, smell and taste. Omit no details: record everything!

Sensory activity 3: notice 5-4-3-2-1. In this activity you will bring your awareness separately to each of your five senses. A mindfulness approach that brings your focus to each of your senses one at a time is helpful in the moment, especially if you are currently experiencing a difficult situation and may be feeling uneasy or anxious about things. Notice 5-4-3-2-1 is a good mindfulness exercise to help you stay grounded in the here and now.

- Find a quiet, private space for you to sit and relax for 5 or 10 minutes.
- Find five things in your room that you can see and describe each object in vivid detail. If you are looking at your lazy-dazed dog snoring on the bed, pay attention to the colors of his coat, the way his belly moves up and down and the shape of his body. There may be other things for you to notice in the

room such as textures, edges, changes in light and the movement of objects.

○ Identify four sounds coming from inside or outside the room; it might help if you close your eyes. Sounds may be coming from a music speaker, fluorescent lighting or the humming of a computer. You may notice sounds coming from the rustling of tree branches, the wind or people talking. Describe these sounds in detail.

○ Identify three things you are touching. What pressure do you feel on your bottom side as you sit in a chair or on the floor? What temperature are you sensing: coolness or warmth? Which objects feel hard on your skin and which feel soft?

○ Take in the odors around you. Are they coming from the kitchen or hallway? Do you smell the scent of perfume or fresh flowers? Identify two smells and describe them.

○ Describe the one single taste you sense at this moment, paying attention to your mouth, lips, inner cheeks, tongue and saliva.

EXERCISE 2:
PRACTICE DAILY MEDITATION

Meditation is central to mindfulness and is a common technique prescribed by psychologists and referred by lifestyle coaches. Let me add that it gets great reviews by its followers. It is easy to see why, as just 5 to 10 minutes of alone time per day to connect with your mind is all you need to reduce the stress hormones of adrenaline and cortisol. Besides, there is no need to trot over to a public facility or gym, which makes meditation easy to implement from home. You don't need any materials except for a quiet space and a comfortable floor mat.

The best way to learn about meditation is to give it a try. Let's do a simple, five-step breathing meditation together.

Step 1: find a comfortable spot on a mat or rug on the floor in a personal space that is free from people talking and other noises. Meditation can be done in a comfy chair or couch but it is ideal to sit on the floor, as the feel of fabric and pillows on your back and arms might feel constricting and distracting. Close your eyes if you think you might get side-tracked by irrelevant sights and sounds from the room.

Step 2: focus on your breathing. Bring your awareness inward and breathe naturally for a minute or two. As you breathe in, remind yourself that you are taking in oxygen that is vital for your internal tissues. When you expel air you are doing something good for your body too: removing toxic carbon dioxide.

Step 3: take deeper breaths. Make the breathing deeper than before, starting with a long, slow breath inward. Notice cool air entering your nostrils. Both lungs are expanding when you take in air and your chest rises, and your lower abdominal cavity shrinks as the air travels into your lungs. Breathe out slowly and evenly, following the air as it leaves your body. Pay attention to your chest collapsing downward as oxygen is released. Be sure when both taking in air and releasing it that you do so slowly. It might help to count inward at a slow pace – one, two, three, four – and then outward slowly – one, two, three, four.

Step 4: your attention is drifting, so bring it back. When you notice your attention shifting to something other than your breathing, gently circle back to your breath. Never feel bad or irritated when your attention shifts, as it is normal for your attention to move freely and it would not be fair if you expected your thoughts to not wander at all. Accept that your thoughts drift in a natural way and be willing to bring them back to the moment. Remember that any time you shift attention in a deliberate way you are taking control of your thoughts without somebody else giving you support or assistance. It is good for you to have this control.

Step 5: continue to attend to your breath and bodily movements. Notice what is happening in your body as you inhale and exhale. Watch how your body's movements and sensations change over the course of the exercise. Is your breath deeper than before? Is it getting easier to release oxygen from your chest? Continue noticing until the meditation period is over.

Meditation gives you control over your thoughts and brings you calm and peace. You may wish to do a google search to explore other kinds of meditation: spiritual, loving-kindness and so on. Regardless of the type of meditation you choose, here are some tips to make meditation easier to do, especially if this is your first time.

SET A REMINDER	To help you remember to meditate at a regular time each day, put a reminder on your phone or post a sticky note on the fridge. It is easy to say you will commit, but forgetting just once can lead to giving up.
START WITH A SHORT MEDITATION	For the first time start with a 2-minute meditation and slowly increase the duration. Typical exercises last anywhere from 5 to 10 minutes.
BE PATIENT WITH YOUR ABILITY TO FOCUS	Take your time, be patient and let your mindfulness occur organically. Gently bring your attention back to where you want it to be, and be prepared to do this several times in one sitting.
TRY GUIDED MEDITATION FOR SUPPORT	In silent meditation you need no one but yourself and quiet space. Guided meditation involves another person, a coach or therapist who will give instructions either in person or virtually.

KNOW WHEN MEDITATION IS HELPFUL . . . OR NOT

Meditation is encouraged for all, adults and children alike, but it is a good idea to shelve this strategy if you suffer from severe anxiety and have big trouble focusing. Before meditating is of value I suggest educating yourself on your inner alarm system and riding out anxious distress (see Chapter 11).

C
H
A
P
T
E
R
—
9

NOTE YOUR
THANKS

*What separates privilege from
entitlement is gratitude.*

– ACADEMIC, PUBLIC SPEAKER AND AUTHOR BRENÉ BROWN

'm not always sincere when I say "Thank you," as sometimes it is a simple reflex to utter the words and at other times I'm attempting to remain polite in social circles. Such as, for example, this morning when I waited in line at the coffee shop drive-through for a good half hour. When I finally made it to the cashier's window, even the retail worker seemed less than enthusiastic about the barrage of customers and relentless exchange between cash and a bag of donut holes. I suspect mockery was not what I intended when I curtly spoke the words "Thank you." After all, both the employee and I got the short end of the stick and we both had good reasons to be irritated with the process involved in this so-called quick-serve restaurant. Without much thought, I hurried a less-than-sincere gesture of acknowledgement, causing me to push forward and producing a chain reaction of cars creeping along the long queue.

At other times, though, I am quite deliberate and thoughtful in noting my thanks. I feel the privilege when something good happens to me. Last year I got the front bumper of my convertible stuck on a cement curb in the parking lot. It was late at night, I was alone and I decided to call my friends, a lovely couple, for help to scrape the car out of this mess. They traveled some distance to my rescue with no hesitation, and naturally I said "Thank you" – several times, actually. I had the same warm feeling the next day when the auto mechanic who assessed the damage concluded that the car's undercarriage was fine. The automobile's bumper was displaced and he promised not to charge too much for new bolts and minimal labor. In both of these scenarios, expressing my gratitude made me feel good, because I was being thankful to those who made a difference to the way I was thinking and feeling.

In the last chapter we looked at two mindfulness approaches for restoring calm and peace into your life: attending to the five senses and practicing meditation. In this chapter we cover two other approaches, each of which involves making notes: putting thoughts and feelings on paper to show how you feel about someone or something. It feels good to appreciate, to feel happy.

EXERCISE 1:
WRITE A GRATITUDE LETTER

Find some private space for thinking and writing, then craft a letter to someone who has made a positive impact in your life such as a relative, employer, former schoolteacher or even an old beau. What you received need not be expensive or rare, and it need not be a material thing at all.

Keep the letter short and sweet, worrying less about grammar and more about what you want to say. The actions and attitude of the person you have in mind do not have to be extraordinary things that happened, and they may have impacted you in more than one way. Because this special person left you feeling strong emotions, it is good to let them know they were not forgotten. It will also help if you add something about what you are up to now.

Writing and delivering gratitude letters are powerful ways to stay mindful. What you are doing is being aware of people and things that influenced you even if you might have forgotten about their impact until now. You will feel empowered even if you go through the effort of writing but never send the letter, because the key here is the process of writing and staying grounded in the moment. This process itself leads to happiness and that is what counts. When you write your gratitude letter, don't forget to:

- include your full name and address and the date
- start the letter politely, with "Dear _____"
- describe specific behaviors and your emotional reaction
- keep the letter brief; one page is sufficient
- sign your letter.

When you have finished your note of thanks, drop it off in a mailbox or email it. You may wish to deliver it in person and have a friendly conversation with your special person. Sometimes people write a letter of gratitude as a memorial intended for someone who has passed. Remember, it can be sent to its recipient or not sent at all, or perhaps you will store the letter for safekeeping or shred it later. The choice is yours.

EXERCISE 2:
THE HAPPINESS PRACTICE

This short exercise will bring you to a positive frame of mind. The happiness practice is customized from exercises in positive psychology, the scientific study of traits that aim to improve your quality of life. You might have come across similar mindfulness strategies, such as the what went well daily journaling exercise or the three good things exercise.

I completed the happiness practice this morning: I sat in my personal space and thought about three things that made me happy today. I did not rush through the exercise, and nor did I do the exercise in my head. Instead, I grabbed a pen and paper and jotted down three items along with reasons why they made me happy. These were my entries:

- I was grateful to have had a friendly Zoom chat with my dear friend Ramaswamy. He seemed animated talking with me, and this made me feel special.
- I was proud that Toula, my devoted chihuahua, nicely followed commands for "Sit" and "Heel" and I am indebted to the puppy classes we did last month.
- I was lucky to have taken a breath of air just now. My breathing was effortless and deep and it made me grateful that I have good health.

Now that you have seen my example of three things that made me happy and why, it's your turn:

THREE THINGS THAT MADE ME HAPPY TODAY
1.
2.
3.

Record in a journal or on a word processor three aspects of your life at this moment that make you feel happy or grateful. The items can be small in importance. Organize your answers by numbering the items 1, 2 and 3 and briefly explain why each item made you feel good. Try doing this exercise once per day, each day choosing a different time to note your thanks. Today you might note your thanks midmorning, and tomorrow you might do it in the evening after work. The following day you might find three things that made you happy when you wake up and start a fresh pot of coffee. You might be thinking it's impossible to come up with three positive things first thing in the morning, but this is what you should strive for. I challenge you to stay mindful about all that is good in your life right now – *in the moment*.

Is the happiness practice simple to do? Not always. If you are feeling sad and unhopeful then chances are you will interpret events in a negative way and it might be hard to find things that are good in your life. When the happiness exercise is completed by people who are depressed there is a tendency to produce, at most, only one single item. Depressed people are being honest when they say that nothing in their life is making them feel grateful, but this is all the more reason why practice is needed. The happiness practice changes your mood by helping you see things in a more positive light.

I wondered if the exercise might be hard to grasp. Well, I doubt the task is overly difficult, because even young children with a short attention span love to rush off a bunch of things that make them happy. Actually, I tried the happiness exercise with my youngest clients, six and seven year olds, and I gave the same exercise to second-year university students in my psychology class. Regardless of age, most found the exercise challenging the very first time but it did get easier. After practicing the happiness exercise for one week students started appreciating smaller things in day-to-day life, and each day it was easier to come up with things that made them happy.

Keep up the happiness practice and you will gain a more positive outlook on life. It is all about being conscious of the things that you normally ignore. Look carefully at things that you customarily take advantage of and train your mind to look for small, positive things. This is why university students ended up finding the practice easier to do once they were inclined to notice things they had ignored before: they became more in tune with the beauty in present life. It is something I wish for everyone.

SUMMARY OF FOUR MINDFULNESS APPROACHES

An autopilot mode of thinking is common these days given the demands of work and home life. It is an outcome of our brain ignoring mundane tasks while attending to challenging problems that take more brain power, but being mindful means that we stop ignoring things and we stop the automaticity in our thinking. Enticing your mind to place deliberate attention on objects that are normally ignored in a busy life can be tricky at first, and it will take practice to be able to let go of the bad thoughts swirling in your mind.

Okay, let's review the four mindfulness exercises from the last two chapters:

- taking in the five senses
- practicing daily meditation
- crafting a letter of gratitude
- undertaking the happiness practice.

DISTRACT
TO
CALM

Worrying does not take away tomorrow's
troubles. It takes away today's peace.

– AMERICAN POET RANDY ARMSTRONG

Are you undergoing a difficult period in your life? Has a bad situation made you feel anxious? If this describes you, the best you can do is manage extraordinary times with a sense of calm, strength and resolve, but right now you may be worlds away from feeling serene or strong. I've been asked more times than I can count: "How do I get rid of my worries? My anxiety doesn't go away no matter what I do."

Anxious distress is something all of us experience at one time or another when we entertain catastrophic thoughts about the future. Physiological distress is what you get inside your body when you have a panic attack. Anyone can be affected big time by internal sensations even if they have never been diagnosed with a panic or anxiety disorder. What is your typical response? An automatic reaction is to dull achy feelings as fast as possible and the natural human response is to run away from bad feelings and push anxiety far, far away. Why do we run from anxiety? We work hard to eliminate distress mainly because:

- intense sensations are unpleasant
- intrusive thoughts and jittery feelings interfere with getting things done.

Although the preference is to run, we can't actually remove ourselves from anxiety because intense sensations are sitting and brewing inside our bodies. If you try to run away, anxiety follows. Some people blunt intense emotions and negative thinking by gulping a stiff drink, lighting a smoke, snacking on chocolate and potato chips or taking some pain pills. I assume you have tried some of these things and that many are within easy reach at home. Having a drink, smoking a cigarette and snacking are escape behaviors and they have the uncanny ability to take away painful feelings . . . well, sort of.

Drugs, alcohol and sugary treats do a lot to reduce feelings of worry and sadness and can be powerful in getting rid of intense anger and frustration – but only temporarily. Not to mention they have serious repercussions for your health. No matter how much you suppress it, upset builds up once substances and the sugar rush wear off.

What can you do for yourself when you have anxiety and distress? I have a few strategies to suggest, and each has been used in therapy to help people manage strong emotions. Both have been known to give relief, although I must admit that one of the strategies seems to work better in the long run. The other strategy may be considered a temporary solution. Regardless, either of the two methods described in the next two chapters is a better option compared with unhealthy coping methods such as over-drinking, eating junk food or using tobacco and marijuana.

One class of treatment is known as distraction techniques, which we will talk about in this chapter. Distraction techniques are commonly used by therapists, so you may have some familiarity with them already. The other technique, feel the feelings or riding out anxiety, is not as common an approach but I believe it is superior because it helps overcome anxiety in the long term. Feel the feelings works well when there is recurrent anxiety that does not seem to let up and is presented in Chapter 11. Review both strategies to see which would be most helpful given your own circumstances and preferences.

DISTRACTION TECHNIQUES

Shelve your anxiety. If anxiety is getting in the way of you getting work done, you can shelve it for a period of time and promise to get back to the negative feelings later. Okay, note here: I am asking you to metaphorically put anxiety on a shelf and make yourself return to bad feelings at a later time, which will likely give you no consolation. Trust me when I say you probably won't need to revisit the anxious feelings at a later point, because then you'll be well on your way to doing other things and you will have forgotten about the incident or can look at a it from a different perspective.

For example, let's say you are sitting at your office desk trying to get tasks completed but your anxiety is so strong it is preventing you from focusing on your work. In this case, your job needs to get done so you promise yourself to shelve the anxiety until later, when you have more time to dwell on negative thoughts and feelings. You may decide to ignore anxiety at 10.00 am (while working) with a pledge to yourself that you will go back, open the imaginary box and experience anxiety at precisely 5.00 pm that same day once you are back home from the office. It is arbitrary what times you choose for putting away anxiety and allowing yourself to bring it back to the forefront of your mind; simply having a delay helps overcome the anxiety. By shelving anxiety you will begin to understand that the power to control it comes from within. When you are ready later to feel the anxiety there is a very good chance the anxiety will have subsided.

Divert your attention. What if you find it difficult to shelve your anxiety, even for a few minutes? Sometimes thoughts can be intrusive and anxiety is way too high. If this describes your feelings, I recommend easy-to-do diversion methods to ward off distress in the moment. These methods work quickly to make you more relaxed and you can do them in the comfort of your home, or you can use them even when you are out and about and wish not to be burdened by strong, annoying feelings. Take a look at the following examples of diversion to calm yourself down quickly and lower anxiety:

- take deep breaths
- listen to music
- tidy up your home
- talk to a friend
- take a long walk
- undergo vigorous exercise
- cuddle your pet
- draw or paint.

Listening to music or calming sounds such as beach waves and rain or visually focusing on a single spot on the wall are quick ways to distract yourself from feelings of distress. Doodling or coloring, counting things around you, counting backward and visualizing a fun game or sport are other ways to distract yourself from unwanted, negative feelings. None of these methods are health hazards; in fact, therapists swear by them if you are struggling with emotions and cannot easily stop your mind from spinning out of control.

In Chapter 8 I introduced you to the mindfulness strategy notice 5-4-3-2-1, which involves bringing your awareness separately to each of your five senses and can be used now. To recap: find five things you see around you, then four things you hear, three things you are feeling, two things you can smell and one thing you can taste. Bringing your focus to each of your senses one at a time will allow you to take your mind away from a stressful situation and any physiological worries.

Practice deep breathing. By practicing deep breathing you will be able to ignore negative thoughts and distract yourself from underlying distress. Some interesting facts about abdominal breathing: it is by far the most common relaxation technique recommended by health practitioners and is a skill used frequently in cognitive behavior therapy, although it goes by different names:

Deep breathing $=$ abdominal breathing
$=$ diaphragmatic breathing

How is deep breathing different from just plain and simple *regular* breathing? Breathing at a normal rate takes in oxygen at a regular pace and delivers it to your body parts for the growth of your tissues and good muscle performance. You have been doing this your entire life, so nothing new, right? When you consciously take the time to breathe deeply and fully, the process does something spectacular: deep or abdominal breathing sends hormones to your muscles rapidly, helping them reduce tension, and causes a change in your physiological state. In other words, it does a little more than just distract you, also helping to lower anxious distress inside. Deep breathing is easy enough and can be done anywhere and any time.

Diaphragmatic breathing is a fancy way of describing what is happening internally when you breathe deeply. Your diaphragm is a thin muscle that separates your chest and lungs from your abdominal cavity. As you inhale slowly your diaphragm contracts and flattens out somewhat, pulling air into your lungs. As you deliberately exhale slowly your diaphragm relaxes and all of that air pushes out of your lungs completely. Do not exhale quickly, because it would otherwise give the opposite effect. If you were to exhale quickly your muscles are not relaxing, and instead of feeling relaxed you would start feeling more aroused and light-headed. Therefore, it is essential to breathe in and out slowly for this strategy to have the desired effects. Four or five deep breaths are all you need to start feeling calm. Easy.

Follow these five simple steps for diaphragmatic breathing:

- Find personal, quiet space. Sit on the floor or in a comfortable chair or lie down if that helps you stay focused on your breaths.
- Place your right hand on your chest and your left hand on your lower abdomen. Placing your hands like this will help you feel what is going on inside when air gets pulled inside your chest and when air gets released slowly.
- Breathe in slowly, counting to four or five. Gradually fill your chest cavity with air. Notice that your right hand is moving upward as your chest expands. Your lower abdomen pushes downward and your left hand moves downward.
- Breathe out slowly. Count to four or five until all of the air has been released. Note that your right hand is moving downward while your left hand moves upward.
- Continue this deep breathing for 5 to 10 minutes. Use deep breathing whenever you want to calm down.

DISTRACTION HELPS . . . FOR A WHILE

Distraction techniques are simple tools to momentarily take your mind away from the underlying problem. This is what happens when you listen to calming sounds, exercise, focus on nice scenery or attend to a picture hanging on the wall. For the most part, quick calming methods do not eliminate anxiety forever.

Once you stop distracting yourself you may notice that anxiety reappears, and more often than not it will come back sooner than you would like. People who are diagnosed with an anxiety disorder understand this all too well. My clients with anxiety have learned the up-and-down cycle of anxiety: they know the waves of anxiety.

Here is an example of how distraction had limited benefit for someone with severe anxiety. Annalise, a 26-year-old store clerk, decided to quit psychotherapy because she found it unhelpful for lowering her anxiety. No matter how much Annalise practiced breathing, her anxiety was through the roof. She had anxiety about many things: her health, job and relationship with her boyfriend. No matter how hard she focused on a pretty picture or the sound of rain, she found it hard to ignore anxiety-provoking situations and the people in her life.

She had rapid breathing and automatic thoughts and she found them to be debilitating.

Luckily, there was another way for Annalise to deal with her anxiety that she would need to try when she was alone. Instead of distracting her mind from what was going on inside, she went to the other extreme: she attended to the internal sensations and gained a better understanding about why they were present in the first place. She learned not to fear underlying physiological sensations and run away from them despite how strong they felt at times. As you can see, this approach is radically different from distraction. It is called the "feel the feelings strategy" and we will turn to it in the next chapter.

THE
ANXIETY
CURE

The only way out is through.

— AMERICAN POET ROBERT FROST

Feel the feelings, or riding out anxiety, is the strategy I recommend if you need to seriously tone down your strong emotions. Feel the feelings involves consciously attending to internal bodily sensations and to the negative thoughts swirling around your mind. It involves dealing with negative feelings as they occur in the moment and understanding why they are there. Rather than ignoring the feelings and hoping for the best, you do the opposite by staying grounded with internal sensations until you get used to them. Eventually, strong emotions drop away: for good. Or, at least, for the most part.

To help you differentiate this strategy from distraction methods such as walking, listening to music or breathing deeply, take a look at its key features:

- You are not being asked to ignore distress by taking deep breaths.
- You are not being asked to ignore distress by other means; for example, focusing on a spot on the wall or listening to rain sounds or soft music.
- You are being asked to stay focused on anxious feelings until they subside. This might take a while, so be patient with the process.

There is a reluctance to ride out anxiety. People who hear about the feel the feelings strategy often say it cannot possibly work for them and think it is impossible to sit with uncomfortable feelings and sensations, but let me tell you: it does work, and it has long-standing positive effects. Feel the feelings as a strategy to ward off anxiety works despite the initial uneasiness it produces. Therefore, it is worth the time you invest in it.

I have used this approach many times with clients who suffer from an anxiety disorder, but it's not just for people diagnosed with that and is easy to implement on your own at home by following these five steps:

- Find personal space.
- Visually scan for danger.
- Focus on body sensations.
- Ride out anxious feelings (note: this might take a while).
- End the exercise when your anxiety subsides.

We turn now to a detailed explanation of each of the five steps as I want you to understand the underlying process. Do not skip the details below, because understanding what is happening to your body and mind is a huge reason why the strategy works so well. Also, I think reading the explanation below will make the instructions easier to follow.

FIND PERSONAL SPACE

The trick to making the feel the feelings strategy work is to have a private space for the exercise. Look for a quiet, comfortable space free from distractions. The timing is not ideal for riding out anxiety if you are expected to do important work at the same time or if you are looking after an infant or rambunctious toddler.

When you are ready for the exercise, go to your personal space. You should not be able to overhear conversations or see what others are doing and you should not be interrupted. Make sure your haven has a comfortable chair or couch. An oversized beanbag chair is just as effective as a bunch of pillows thrown on the floor. The room should be an ideal temperature – not too warm or too cold – otherwise you will end up being distracted from the task.

VISUALLY SCAN FOR DANGER

Once you have secured some personal space, pay attention to your surroundings. Start with moving your head from side to side and visually scan for any threats. This is a simple way to quickly discover that all is well and that there is nothing bad going on in your surroundings. Recognize that you are panicking about something that is not truly a threat to your survival.

You need to understand the reasoning behind looking for danger. There is an upside of anxiety: physiological distress is a warning sign that something is wrong and that you must *not* ignore it. It is a perfectly sound alarm system that is a survival mechanism designed to help you escape a dangerous situation. It is easier to understand your body's alarm system by comparing it to animals in the wild. Imagine a deer being stalked by a ferocious wolf. The deer has just noticed a rustle, a sound in the forest. A big feature of the alarm system is sudden rapid breathing combined with a pounding heart, the good ol' sympathetic nervous system working as it should. Justifiably so, the deer escapes the threat of being eaten. The deer has a better chance of getting away from its predator in the presence of a functioning cardiovascular system, one that promotes faster breathing and the delivery of oxygen and other nutrients to the deer's muscles. In this scenario, multiple physiological changes begin one by one to give the submissive animal an opportunity to dart. Here are some examples of those physiological changes:

- The pounding heart ensures that oxygen goes to tissues for speed of movement and strength.
- The digestive system quietens down temporarily, shifting energy to the circulatory system. In humans,

we experience this temporary shutdown in our digestion as nausea, a pit in the stomach or a sudden loss in appetite.

ο Body temperature fluctuates to avoid overheating and collapse. Humans flip from getting the chills to having heat sensations.

ο Pupils widen and hypervigilance sets in as the deer is on the lookout for a stalking wolf. In humans, the effects of larger pupils and being hyper-focused are dizziness and poor concentration, respectively.

There are many more changes that occur inside the body and I could go on with an analogy between the deer and human. The point is this: when you find yourself experiencing distress you have the same physiological reactions as a deer – *but do you have the same threat?*

All animals engage in protective action. Humans are a special species insofar as we come equipped into this world with a smart brain, the cerebral cortex, that we might overuse on occasion. What I am saying is that sometimes you think way too much for your own good. Recall what happens inside when you envision that a threat is looming. You might obsess over the bad event even when no threat exists, and you'll probably continue to worry and feel worse even when nothing really bad is happening.

The thinking brain mistakenly causes the body to activate the alarm system by courtesy of the sympathetic nervous system. This error happens a lot, particularly when your thoughts are running out of control and are irrational and unhelpful. A therapist or friend can help you see the irrational thinking that led to the alarm system tripping out, but we can only do so much. It is your alarm and you need to learn for yourself how to control uncomfortable internal sensations.

Scanning for danger is a critical step that cannot be done quickly; you cannot gloss over this step. By scanning for danger you are drawing attention to why the alarm system has been activated in the first place, then by looking around you are proving that nothing bad is happening and you must get to the bottom of the bad feelings inside. Remember that in a relaxed state of mind you would look at the situation differently and convince yourself that everything is in fact all right. The key is to get yourself in this better frame of mind.

FOCUS ON BODY SENSATIONS

You have just scanned for danger and found none, so now stop attending to the world around you – the sounds in the house, the brightness or darkness of the room, the memories of conversations you just had. Close your eyes, mentally let go of the outside world and bring your focus to the internal workings of your body and mind.

To get started, look and feel within and ask yourself: Is my heart pounding? Am I dizzy or nauseous? Am I shaking? Strong emotions can be agonising, but the discomfort itself is a mere side-effect of your brain telling your body to move from a dangerous place to a safe one. Remember to tell yourself "I'm safe. No worries."

Below are some common sympathetic nervous system responses:

- feeling tense or restless
- a faster heart rate
- rapid breathing
- sweating
- trembling and/or chills
- feeling muscular tiredness
- feeling mentally exhausted
- having trouble concentrating
- stomach upset.

Do not be afraid of these normal physiological responses. Recall the example I gave about the deer running away from its predator and try to understand how physiological changes are important to the deer's survival – and to your own survival.

RIDE OUT ANXIOUS FEELINGS

Continue to stay with uncomfortable internal sensations until they subside. Physiologically, it is impossible for strong bodily sensations to continue forever: believe me when I say they cannot escalate to infinity. It might take a while, so be patient. You must wait for the rollout of biological (chemical) changes to occur in your body.

Naturally, everyone wants to know how long they need to ride out anxiety. I cannot say how long it will take for your body to calm down: it could take 5 minutes, it might take 2 hours, so be prepared to take whatever time is needed. Change happens once you begin to interpret the normal fight/flight response symptoms accurately. You must take control over inner sensations and remind yourself that you are physically fine. Riding out anxiety is the same as de-activating the fight/flight response. In this way, your parasympathetic nervous system kicks in and makes your body more relaxed.

END THE EXERCISE WHEN YOUR ANXIETY SUBSIDES

Eventually, you will no longer feel distress. If you start getting bored then this is a good sign: it means you have adapted and have changed your internal state from bad to neutral. Be prepared to repeat the exercise when physiological sensations creep in at another time. Before you go and explore the world anxiety free, give yourself a gentle squeeze for your bravery in trying something new and helpful.

TIPS FOR MANAGING STRONG EMOTIONS

Do not escape. Never try to escape when you are anxious. Remember that physiological changes inside your body will never hurt you and that your body gets activated only because your brain senses a problem even if danger does not exist.

Be patient. Riding out unpleasant bodily reactions is not easy to do, or not the first time. Your brain needs to recalculate and reinterpret that no physical danger exists, then your body has to start the process of settling down. Of course, the more times you ride out distress the less strong it will be over time. It goes away because of your own efforts.

Take control. Managing anxiety is important to day-to-day functioning, whether you are at work, in school or at home interacting with loved ones. Therapists such as myself can educate you about the human fight/flight response but only you can ward off anxiety, distress and other negative emotions. At the end of the day the best resource for bringing the body back to a stable state is you, the bearer of this intricate, hard-working alarm system. You are the best person to bring your body to a relaxed place. What you are doing is helping your body achieve homeostasis. The only way to achieve success is finding that comfortable space and embracing alone time.

* * *

Mindfulness is about being present; that is, being fully aware of what is happening within and around you. When you stay mindful you refrain from being overwhelmed by what is happening inside and stop over-reacting to events around you. This is precisely what you are being asked to do in the feel the feelings strategy.

PART III

P
E
R
S
I
S
T

REMOTE WORK MINUS THE STRESS

Without great solitude no serious work is possible.

– PAINTER AND SCULPTOR PABLO PICASSO

I did not know much about remote work until after it became a huge part of my life. Even before the coronavirus pandemic some people found it convenient to do work from a home office, mostly professionals in management, business and finance. Remote work is efficient enough as long as you have the type of occupation that allows for it, although the number of people working from home worldwide has skyrocketed since the pandemic.

Minimizing the spread of viral infection is one good reason why some were politely encouraged to work from home, although there are other benefits. You can avoid travel time, rush hour and poor weather conditions. You might be able to get away with wearing casual, comfortable clothes over suits and other formal attire, if that means something to you. At home, there can be fewer distractions and disruptions such as loud noises from machinery and annoying conversations by co-workers. Working from home is a lifesaver for busy working parents who coordinate paperwork and home-care responsibilities during the daytime, such as taking children to a bus stop, driving to school for early pick up or making impromptu medical appointments or visits to the hairstylist and bank. There are many conveniences in working from home, and because of this there is every reason to believe that remote work is here to stay.

There are also some pitfalls when trying to do work from home. Have you felt frustrated by the lack of materials available? Were you ever perturbed by a slower network? Is your home environment even safe? These are some challenges described by home workers:

- It is hard to maintain a boundary between work and home life.
- I don't have the right materials to complete work from home.
- I have no one to talk to and I miss my co-workers.
- I'm not getting enough support or advice from a supervisor.
- I am working too much; I feel like I'm working all the time.

The need to maintain optimal health and wellness when working from home is paramount given the digital world in which we live. Try these recommendations if remote work is something you are doing now or plan to do some time in the future:

- find personal space for work
- create work/life boundaries

- build in ergonomics
- develop self-learning skills.

FIND PERSONAL SPACE FOR WORK

It is good to find personal space and some solitude when spending work time at home. If personal devices are not necessary to do your job, turn them off. Move your cell phone out of reach and avoid constant text messages and non-urgent emails from friends and colleagues. These are distractors that make it hard to finish important tasks and often lead to errors.

A good way to avoid distractions is to secure a room with a door. I realize a special room dedicated for work is not feasible for everyone and that whether or not you have one will depend on the size of your home and on whether you must accommodate family members. Sometimes it is hard to negotiate personal space with family members who also need their own space, but try to find some space such as a room or spot far away from common areas just for you.

Privacy is helpful in order to create boundaries between work tasks and those activities and people we associate with in home life. A separate room or quiet location away from the spouse, children and family pets is helpful if you are the type of person who gets easily distracted.

Be watchful of loud conversations, the sound from TV, general noise levels and air temperature. These are often overlooked, but extreme levels of noise and temperature have been known to lessen productivity and make workers feel less satisfied with work.

What do you need to do in order to minimize distractions from home?

CREATE WORK/LIFE BOUNDARIES

Working from home can lead to longer hours of work time. That was no typo: *longer* hours. Suppose you ordinarily work from 9 to 5 at the office, which adds up to roughly seven or eight hours of work time per day. At home, work time might very well jump to nine, ten or more hours. I know; it sounds illogical. It happens when you want to make a good impression on your boss and may wish to show that you are a responsible employee who takes work seriously. Perhaps you are proving to yourself and your colleagues that you are disciplined enough to perform job duties from a less formal home office, that you are the type of person who won't slack off and be distracted by other things. If this is you, then you are not alone. What happens is that people who work from home generally want to ensure they stay on top of work matters, and they sometimes blur the line between work time and leisure time.

I distinctly remember this being the case for me early in my career. At the time my three kids were in elementary school. I started my workday in my home office around 7.00 am with coffee in hand, knowing that I would break at noon to make a hot lunch for me and the children and then walk them back to school. However, leaving work to prepare lunch and get everyone back in work mode made me realize that I was taking valuable time away from a demanding job. Can you actually believe I felt guilty spending more time with my family and less time on the job? To make up for what I saw as lost work time I got back to the computer for a few hours later in the evening once the kids finished their homework and were ready for bed. This meant that, technically, work time for me ended up being 12 hours per day. Of course, that routine did not last long as I became overtired and depressed. Eventually I solved the problem by learning to work fewer hours per day and making room for more me time and family time.

Think carefully about how much time you devote to work each day. Research shows that when workload jeopardizes leisure time and interferes with caregiving, the result is higher reports of work dissatisfaction, depression and burnout. Therefore, you may want to consider using a schedule or calendar and determine the boundary between work time and break time. Speak to your employer if you feel you have a crazy busy workload. It is important to make changes now and create a better work/life balance.

Breaks taken throughout the workday are necessary to recharge. I cannot stress enough the need for physical activity and mind breaks. Break time is the perfect time to check social media and stay connected with other people. If you do the majority of your work at home, ask your employer to incorporate virtual lunch meetings so you can stay connected with co-workers.

BUILD IN ERGONOMICS

Watch for muscle pain and injuries stemming from poor posture and sitting for long periods in front of a computer screen. Neck and back injuries are brought on by non-ergonomic office equipment.

Ergonomics is nothing new in the worplace, and companies worldwide invest millions in ergonomic equipment and devices. Ergonomic chairs support the upper limbs and neck and prevent back injuries in desk workers. Special keyboard devices support the wrists and arms and prevent carpal tunnel syndrome. Sit-stand desks are fairly new pieces of office equipment, the purpose of having these moveable desks being to give you a chance to adjust your posture. Moving from sit-down to stand-up positions provides better circulation of your blood to body tissues, burns more calories and gives you more energy. Don't forget regular exercise throughout the workday, which reduces pain, boosts your mood, and lowers anxiety and stress.

Most organizations do a fairly decent job of implementing ergonomics in the workplace, but while more and more people are doing work from home I am incredulous that occupational health and safety is largely being overlooked. What is lacking is an assessment of the physical work conditions in people's homes: employers who ask employees to work from home do not generally ask about the set-up of workstations that belong to their employees. Employees may not even realize the potential for health problems due to poorly designed equipment and being inactive for the majority of the workday, nor does the average person necessarily know that musculoskeletal disorders of the bone, tendons and muscles develop slowly over time.

It is a sad reality that soft-tissue injuries are hard to correct if left untreated. My advice is that if you are a frequent computer user you should take the initiative in home-office ergonomics. Also, watch for good body posture and movements (see Chapter 5 for a detailed discussion about good posture). For intense computer work or if you are writing for long periods:

- Use an ergonomic chair.
- Your computer monitor should be 2 feet from your face, with the top of the screen placed at eye level. Position the screen upward slightly; that is, 10 degrees, to avoid tilting your head too high or too low.
- Avoid leaning against a headboard or sitting against a wall. These positions put your head in a forward tilt and put strain on your neck and upper shoulders.
- Avoid using a laptop on your lap. (I know, it needs a better name!)
- Use a timer on your desk or phone to remind you to take a break. Take a break from the same position after an hour or so.
- Try a height-adjustable standing desk and alter your position from time to time. Make sure that both feet are flat on the floor and that you are not slouching; a foot rest can be an asset. The benefits of standing include burning more calories and maintaining a higher energy level.

If you are a manager or business owner make a genuine commitment to improve the health and safety of your employees. Be prepared to conduct an assessment of the needs of each employee who works from home. My thought is that if organizations want you to work from home they should be investing time and funds to ensure a safe and healthy working space. You, as the employee, should identify problems and bring them to the attention of your employer. Take a proactive approach by inviting your boss to evaluate your personal workspace, and figure out what materials and resources will improve your home-working environment.

DEVELOP SELF-LEARNING SKILLS

Because of remote work we have had to to change how we do job tasks. I eliminated face-to-face therapy sessions with clients and learned how to use a videoconferencing platform as a way to deliver health care. Teletherapy, doing medical visits and psychotherapy virtually from home have now become common practice for health-care practitioners. As you can imagine, the move to teletherapy was not easy to do for an old gal who was not brought up with digital technology; learning how to use Zoom for patient calls required a fair bit of self-teaching.

Self-teaching or self-learning (or retraining) is the way to be successful in remote work. You really have to be able to work on your own and you have to be actively involved and interested in learning new things. There is no supervisor, no lead hand, no helpful co-worker who can walk you through tasks. Working from home, then, means you will need good focus and concentration. You must be able to ignore irrelevant distractions that occur at home.

Much of what we know about self-directed learning comes from research in education. Education researchers Michael Barbour and Thomas Reeves noted that good grades came from students who took the initiative in doing schoolwork, who were motivated to excel, who monitored their performance and who had fairly good time-management skills, among other strengths. These are the very characteristics that make up self-learning and are found in self-regulated learners.

Self-regulation is the ability to control your thoughts and actions in order to achieve work goals. It is as important for learners as it is for stay-at-home workers. Each of us is responsible for independently organising materials and activities, following through with goals and staying on top of job tasks. If you are a remote worker or plan to do work from home in the future, you will need to ask yourself how good you are at regulating your behaviors. Answer these questions about your self-regulation skills:

- Do I know how to track my progress?
- What resources are available to me to finish work from home? In case I need help, who/what do I turn to: email a supervisor, call a co-worker for help or perhaps undertake a quick google search for information?
- What motivates me to work harder?
- What types of rewards help me to get tasks started?
- What motivates me to get work finished?
- Do I have the stamina to stay on task for long periods?
- Am I the kind of worker who takes reasonable breaks in an effort to manage my workload?

Boost your self-regulation skills through things such as changing your routine and stopping unhelpful patterns of behavior, and figure out which materials you need to monitor your performance and modify job tasks. It's a good idea to practice setting achievable goals; you may wish to ask your employer to help you with goal setting.

One more thing: workers who are confident and capable in adapting to home-office work also say they have been supported by upper management and had good communication with their superiors for setting realistic goals. If you feel supported and heard by the company you work for then surely this is a good sign that the organization is committed to your well-being, which is a great thing.

SUMMARY

At the time I was fully immersed in writing this chapter on remote work I remembered many jurisdictions had eased Covid restrictions and allowed people to go back to the workplace, at least for a portion of their time, in what is considered our new normal. However, the reality is that no one is really sure whether future COVID-19 outbreaks might change (again) the way citizens and employees conduct their business and besides, in recent years many organizations permitted greater overlap between home and work.

Toggling between the workplace and home office is designed to improve productivity and job satisfaction. Given our changing world, I strongly suggest we stay vigilant and seek optimal health and safety. I believe more discussion is needed on what happens in the environment of the worker when switching from the workplace to a personal home office.

Workers today are juggling a myriad of tasks. As you transition from workplace to home office you may be missing much-needed materials and self-learning skills. In this chapter I offered recommendations in four areas that I believe are in need of attention during changing and challenging times: creating personal space for work, making time for breaks and work/life balance, introducing ergonomics at the home office and developing self-learning skills. It is not just your own responsibility to maintain good health at your job. You are not alone, and organizations need to respect employees' home life and be responsible for teaching how to achieve health and safety conditions at home – which is a sure sign of their commitment to you, their employee.

HIT THE BOOKS AND SELF-TEACH

If kids can be super engaged in video games, there's a way for them to be super engaged in education as well.

– BUSINESS MAGNATE ELON MUSK

Picture a log schoolhouse with large windows, a row of wooden desks, a chalkboard and one tall lectern at front and center. This is what I conjure up when I think of the Westmorland County Grammar School in rural New Brunswick, Canada, where my great-grandmother, Sadie Robb, held her place of employment as the dame school mistress. For my granny this was where you got educated in the late 1800s.

Who would have imagined that looking forward into the 21st century, schools are only one approach for delivering formal education. Education that happens away from a bricks and mortar classroom is known as distance education or distance learning. In my youth, distance university courses saw me receiving by snail mail a bin of binders and a box of audio cassettes. The weekly cassettes with lectures are what I used in my father's ancient but reliable tape recorder, but that was a long time ago when correspondence courses by mail were trending. I am pretty sure this is not what you were thinking about when I mentioned distance learning.

How does distance education take place these days? The internet, due to its fast-developing telecommunications bandwidth capabilities, has become the modern way in which learning takes place from home. Learners log in to a web-based learning management system containing course content, assignments and a calendar of due dates for tests and homework. It is managed by school administers and an IT department. Teachers organize course material into modules and students read text material, watch narrated PowerPoint slides and tune in to interactive content such as video and audio files in their own time.

Electronic mail is the most common method for students and instructors – much like the rest of us – to communicate with one another when separated by physical space and time. Additional online learning tools are added at the discretion of the instructor: chat rooms, threaded discussion boards, messaging apps and videoconferencing. You probably know this interface if you've ever taken courses or helped a student find their way through remote learning.

Speaking of finding your way through remote learning, the pandemic in early 2020 was another phenomenon we would never have imagined, one that resulted in the temporary closure of traditional schools around the world. To control the highly contagious coronavirus, lockdowns were enforced, and more than 1.5 billion children in more than 188 countries worldwide were forced to switch from going to school to doing all of their schoolwork and learning from home. Schools in my vicinity moved to remote learning four times in just two years. The fourth wave was caused by the Omicron surge. In January 2022 I was asked to be interviewed by a news reporter in the city of Waterloo in Ontario and share my views on the effects of remote learning on children. The excerpt below is the beginning portion of that interview.

Robert (the reporter): Thank you for taking my call. As you know, the province of Ontario initiated yet another major lockdown for schools following the recent rise in COVID-19 cases. I wondered if you will participate in a story about a young mother of two who faces rather big challenges with remote learning. The family is feeling frustrated, hopeless even, after all of these lockdowns.

Sybil: Yes, I understand how parents are worried and feeling powerless knowing that their young ones must adapt to remote learning. It takes a mental toll on caregivers, children and teachers when switching back and forth from school to home learning. What's worse, the pandemic is something we are still trying to get a handle on. It is hard to know where to turn for answers.

Robert: The mother I interviewed shared that her son and daughter were disappointed. Actually, depressed was the word they used to describe their feelings. Now, after the fourth wave, they are fed up with missing team sports and not hanging out with school friends. Their mother has concerns of her own: she thinks they are not learning subjects properly from home. She doesn't want her children to miss the basic skills necessary for a college education.

Sybil: We need research to understand the long-term effects of lockdowns and remote learning on education and social development. For now, let's discuss what makes it hard for students to learn remotely, then we should talk about helpful strategies for caregivers and students to make online learning successful.

Robert: Given our reality that the new normal is remote work and remote learning, it does make sense to share useful tips and tools with readers.

Why do people choose online learning? What challenges do students face in remote learning? Are there any strategies to make remote learning successful? I am not here to convince you or your loved one that online learning is above all and should be adopted by all, although I emphasize that each of us at one time or another needed to do something important from a home computer under lockdown. Therefore, it is worth reading on if you will be registering for online courses, if you are a user already or if you are a caregiver and wish to help someone who is doing remote learning. By the way, these days there are so many ways to describe remote learning. I am using the terms remote learning, at-home learning, online learning, e-learning and distance education interchangeably.

DISTANCE LEARNING IS ON THE UP AND UP

Online offerings are a great marketing strategy. Colleges and universities boost enrolment by adding online courses to their traditional suite of classroom courses, and schools make good income by having more people sign up for in-class and distance courses. They also increase profits while serving a demographic of users who are savvy when it comes to technology.

For mature adults with responsibilities outside of school – that is, childcare or a full-time career – the biggest advantage is the convenience about when learning takes place. Online education is an ideal option if you wish to enrol in university but cannot make it to campus during daytime hours, when most courses are offered in person. When you learn from home you can avoid traveling to and from campus and have no hassles with traffic and no need to search for parking on campus.

Here are some reasons why people like the option of online learning:

○ Completing coursework and finishing courses at their own pace, which is important given their demanding professions.
○ Accepting an offer of admission to an academic program they've always wanted to do without needing to relocate to a new city.
○ Avoiding travel time, especially because they have home and work responsibilities to deal with during the day.

TRICKY ISSUES

Internet-based distance education does have some disadvantages. I refer to these problems as "tricky issues," as I expect many students will be motivated enough to compensate for weaknesses in learning style and master some talents in order to study from home. The following list is not comprehensive by any means, but it does give a good idea of certain issues to mull over before embarking on at-home learning. If these potential pitfalls can be overcome the result will be enhancing your learning experience from home.

I can't connect. You must always have access to a device. It would not work well if you didn't have a quiet place to work on the computer. Likewise, problems with the internet provider and network downtime or slow speed interfere with keeping up with assignments and readings, and time-sensitive material. With a slower internet speed you might not finish homework in a timely fashion. These are basic issues to resolve but it is critical to sort them out before committing to online coursework.

I can connect but am not good at keeping up with it. For some the problem is not about not connecting to the network but about developing a routine and learning to connect to the network regularly. You need a routine for doing schoolwork, so be a regular user so you can actively participate in your learning.

Email is probably the most common method these days for communicating quickly with others. Using emails with fellow students and the instructor is useful for getting questions answered, receiving supportive comments and getting prompt feedback on your work. Are you expected to do a group project with a bunch of students? Be sure to get the email addresses of the students in your class with whom you are involved in group work and check your inbox frequently.

I'm not computer savvy. You do not need to be an expert with computers or digital technology to do online coursework. Start with some understanding of the software and educational programs you will be using. Your instructor might ask you to use messaging apps, videoconferencing and threaded discussion boards, not to mention a learning-management system. Familiarize yourself with the interface of online learning and be open and motivated towards new and different ways of learning.

John Sener defined "cyberizing" as the ability to adapt to digital technology and digital culture. He felt that seasoned university instructors (like me!) were not cyberized, and this was not ideal for teaching our students. I would take this one step further and say that all users – students, teachers and parents of students – need to be cyberized if we expect online education to work. First and foremost, being stuck with minimal technological knowledge or skill or being wary or fearful to try technology make it impossible to do your coursework from home despite how fast your internet is at home.

I have no personal space. My best advice time and time again is: **find your personal space**. Your home space for online coursework is more than just physical space. It comprises a physical location and unique domestic aids such as, for instance, a large desk or desk workstation, a beanbag chair for reading in comfort, a whiteboard for brainstorming and bright large windows and plants for stamina and positivity. It may include any number of small tokens or large pieces of furniture that your heart and brain desire to make learning enjoyable. Your learning space at home includes digital space as well, such as screens, websites, mobile apps and the learning-management system. Pay close attention to both physical and digital space.

Take time to evaluate how your own learning space is currently laid out. You might not be able to change a room's paint color and may be limited in the location of your workspace. You may have little control over whether nearby areas are crowded (the kitchen or family room) or dark and isolating (the basement recreation room), but surely some items may be worth adding or replacing to maximize privacy and quietness while at the same time feeling comfortable and energized. If your study area is near a common area used by other family members you may want to consider purchasing a noise-canceling machine or sound conditioner that give off a constant humming sound. The constant hum is quite effective because it masks people talking and other distracting noises.

I lack ergonomics and organisation. Try to choose a desk and office chair that are ergonomically correct. If you can, use more than one desk or opt for a workstation that can house both computer equipment and paper and pencil tools. Be sure to add lighting where you see fit and use natural light if at all possible by opening the blinds and curtains.

Being better organized with office materials will make you more productive. Are there sufficient storage cabinets and shelves to hold books, binders and essential widgets? Can you do away with non-essential gadgets or other distractions such as a nearby mobile phone that might otherwise get in the way of doing work? It might be helpful to add a timetable or schedule and a bulletin board to keep paper clutter off the desk area. Also, cord management is a must for keeping your physical space safe from falls and clutter free.

I need help with self-regulation. Self-regulation skills involve a number of features: actively taking charge of school activities and the learning process, reflecting on how well or how poorly you do in projects and assignments and creating specific, attainable goals in order to succeed. Self-regulation is essential in an online learning environment because you will need to keep up with the momentum of weekly assignments and readings and you will need to follow through with deadlines.

Students at risk of failing in the traditional classroom have poor self-regulation skills. Students who do not do well in online courses and end up dropping out also have trouble self-regulating. Therefore, notice whether you can self-regulate sufficiently or will need to work on this. Decide if there are features or characteristics you would be willing to change. If you are a student, parent or teacher, consider how you might answer the following questions about yourself or a student who wishes to begin online learning:

- Will you follow instructions without assistance, or seek resources to help understand task instructions? To whom could you turn for help, such as the online instructor, internet websites for knowledge or your peers?

- Do you have staying power to work for long periods? Would you be willing to take breaks to help with focus and concentration?

- What motivates you? Will certain types of rewards help get assignments completed? For example, buying a specialty drink at the local cafe, spending 30 minutes of playtime on a new computer game or hanging out with a friend.

_ Can you use a schedule to better manage your time? Would you adopt study materials to meet specific goals?

_ Would you try learning strategies and resources offered by the instructor if they were made available? Do you know how to track your own progress and performance?

I have trouble reading and writing. Online learning requires basic learning skills and may not be a good fit for everyone. It involves a fair amount of reading and the expression of thoughts, ideas and even questions using words, either via email or written assignments. If you dislike writing then distance learning might very well turn into an unpleasant experience. In fact, it is well known that for people who have learning disabilities in reading and written expression, online coursework has been problematic. Keep these points in mind as you decide whether online education is for you.

VIRTUAL SCHOOLS

Online learning has taken off for younger students just as it has been popular for college students and mature adults furthering their professional skills. In what has been dubbed "virtual schools," elementary and high school students work at home while their teacher assigns work and checks in periodically by email. One of the main reasons why parents enrol their children in virtual schools is because of their desire to home school. A second reason reported by parents is that their teenage son or daughter is failing one or more subjects and requires credit recovery.

Do you have a loved one, a child or grandchild struggling with remote learning? What are the ingredients that make at-home or distance learning better for young people?

In distance learning students work on coursework at their own pace. There is no guarantee that any teen will buckle down and be studious at home, but being given a choice about when, how and where they do schoolwork might change a young person's viewpoint about who is responsible for their learning. At-home instruction permits flexibility in terms of when coursework gets done and allows the student to choose when and how many breaks should be taken. Maybe you know a student who has problems with staying focused, especially when it comes to finishing mundane schoolwork, or someone who has a problem following the teacher's rules. Some students perform better when they are not forced to be in a structured, fast-paced classroom. Remote learning takes away the pressure of following class rules.

There are other factors that come into play as to whether online learning works better than traditional classroom learning. Consider personality style or traits: if you know someone who is introverted in character or perhaps socially anxious you might find they prefer learning from home rather than being immersed in a large classroom with other learners. They might actually do better academically once anxiety-provoking social situations are taken out of the mix. Some of my shy and quiet clients tell me they find it intimidating when surrounded by gregarious, happy-go-lucky classmates because they don't like being noticed or judged, which is why they feel less comfortable in a typical school setting compared with when they are working from home. When schools moved to remote learning during the pandemic my shy clients literally felt at home in their learning.

Virtual schools were originally intended to attract bright self-starters who thrived when they could take control of their learning. Does your loved one appear intelligent? Do you feel they would do better academically with less structure and more self-control? Online learning is great for high-achieving, gifted students, who can work efficiently and don't have to put up with less-mature or disruptive classmates. In online instruction it is possible for teachers to give feedback immediately and students can correct their mistakes right away. At the same time, teachers are not micro-managing the activities of their pupils because students decide when they will start their studies and when they will take a break. Besides, smart students tend to spend more time on content that is challenging and interesting, and they usually learn ahead of the average student. These are some great reasons to give young students online options.

The number one goal here is to enhance academic success and a love of learning. See if the points below apply to your loved ones and friends. Online courses are great for students with:

- the desire to be home schooled
- a need for credit recovery or a credit upgrade
- poor classroom attendance, poor adherence to class rules and a risk of dropping out
- a propensity for intellectual stimulation and challenge and working ahead of same-age peers.

DISTANCE LEARNING FOR LIFELONG LEARNING

We learn about things our entire lives, not just until the end of high school or university and not just when we are taking courses as part of professional development or job training. Learning ranges from formal education, job-related training and vocational skills training to refresher courses, general interest courses, and hobbies or other recreational activities. Think about the ways in which you have learned something new today: maybe you developed a special skill at work; perhaps you learned to prepare a new dish; or maybe you read about some great topics by surfing the internet for TED talks, YouTube videos, Wikipedia and so forth.

We live in a globalized world in which technology has advanced quickly. For these reasons it makes sense to stay on top of new information and developments and it is necessary to sharpen our skills and adapt to our ever-changing world. Maybe you've been considering a new occupation, which means learning computer technology and other new skills. Perhaps you are a mature adult with responsibilities at home such as caring for children or grandchildren. Distance learning is a great alternative because you can work through online coursework at your own pace and liking. If you have started retirement you may be looking for online courses to learn about good health and ageing well. Research has shown that elderly learners not only have time to devote to online courses, they also have a keen interest in topics such as the changing climate, health, history and travel.

Take some personal space at home and participate in online learning. You can be educated at home without the need for face-to-face interaction between you and an instructor. There is so much to be educated about. Many universities offer courses for credit, which is a good way to further your expertise and enhance personal development. For older adults, online coursework has been shown to reduce cognitive decline and promote successful ageing, which is important when you consider the fact that the percentage of older adults keeps growing. According to the latest United Nations Report from the Department of Economics and Social Affairs, there are 703 million people in the world aged 65 or older. Today's elderly folks comprise a growing number of people who are driven to stay fit, be active, self-learn, and progress mentally and physically.

Of course, you will need more than just network connectivity and technological tools to make online learning work: personal characteristics play a big role in the success of distance learning. If you are new to online learning, remember to be less guarded and more receptive to trying digital forms of communication such as messaging apps, videoconferencing, threaded discussion boards and the school's learning-management system. Mastery of self-regulation skills is an essential component of distance learning, and once you do that you will be able to transfer self-regulation and self-learning skills to other aspects of your life.

As an illustration, after taking a course via distance learning you may begin to feel more resourceful at locating information on the internet. Likely you will feel comfortable working on your own in front of a computer. Because of your confidence and successes you might decide to apply self-regulation skills in traditional coursework or on the job. You will be less distracted and more likely to finish tasks or jobs because you are better at monitoring and evaluating your own performance.

Learning is integral to life and is something we all seek to continue, and we should do it because our brains are plastic over a lifespan. To say that the brain is plastic or malleable is really saying it has the potential to learn and change into old age. To that end, in today's digital world it is clear that distance learning *and* lifelong learning absolutely go hand in hand.

DISCUSSION QUESTIONS

1. Remember a time when you were a student in high school or at university and there were one or more barriers or obstacles to learning. Think of ways in

which distance learning eliminates or minimizes obstacles to learning.

2. Michelle Harrison, from Thompson Rivers University in Canada, argued that research is needed to map out ideal home conditions to excel in distance education. What do you feel you or your loved one need at home to be successful at online learning? What kinds of things could make online learning easier?

3. After reading this chapter, how would you define self-regulation skills and self-regulated learning? In what other domains outside of education do people self-regulate? Why do you suppose it is important in life?

POSITIVE
INFLUENCES

There is no WiFi in the forest,
but you'll find a better connection.

— ANONYMOUS

You've got to love social media for giving us an array of fitness and nutrition apps to choose from. Public health officials advise that everyone ought to maintain regular physical activity and that we need to persist with fitness goals. For this reason it should not surprise consumers that the number of fitness apps in cyberspace keeps growing – and growing.

Many apps deal with weight loss and many more apps encourage balanced diets and a healthier lifestyle. Remember: I'm the gal who likes her power walking every morning. I found an app that keeps track of how many steps I take per day. To be truthful, I found 20 apps of this type, got confused by the choices and quickly ended the mayhem by closing my eyes and randomly pointing to the one that I am using today, but I did good. Once I enter a walking goal for the week the daily steps app encourages me to work towards it, and every day that's exactly what I do. I like the app mostly because it has a supportive online community of walkers my age.

There are considerable benefits from using fitness apps. You don't have to check the hours of operation of a local fitness center, and you don't need to calculate the travel time to the gym or whether you will need to deal with traffic or poor weather and driving conditions. You don't need to pay out costly membership dues either.

Chapter 4 discussed the huge benefits of doing physical activities in the comfort of your home, but caution is needed when putting faith in social media to meet your fitness goals. I see two potential problems with using social media in order to get fit, both of which are really important issues to deal with when you are using the internet so pay close attention.

First, there is a tendency for people to get addicted when scrolling through videos and fitness forums. As you know by now, scrolling through digital feeds can become an endless endeavour. Digital engineers purposely designed it this way so that naïve consumers get hooked and just keep scrolling. Remember that your goal in doing an internet search is to find ways to get out of your chair and move; your goal is trying to resist being inactive. Watch if you are spending more time trying to find a decent workout than doing the actual workout. Always watch the time you spend surfing the internet when your primary goal is to raise the bar on physical activity.

> **Persist in your goals to stay active
> and fit, and resist sitting around
> scrolling through social media.**

The second potential problem is that the desire to be healthy might backfire because social media is geared towards the perfect body. You might have the best intentions for improving your health but then social media turns on you, and this is what you have to watch out for. Social media has been criticized for leading people down a dark path of unhealthy behaviors such as restricted eating, binge eating and over-exercising to exhaustion and injury.

My 15-year-old neighbor Tammy insists she is into healthy eating. At the same time I can tell by her physique and appearance that she is also very interested in looking pretty and making a good impression. Why not? She is a typical teenager, after all. In any case, Tammy assures me she will never go down the dark path of unhealthy behaviors and I believe her, because I have always known her to be a mature adolescent. However, it is a tad worrisome that my young friend surrounds herself with social media influencers on Twitter, Instagram and TikTok. Social media influencers weren't around when I was a blossoming teen, and it took a while for me to comprehend the idea that young people now have access to thousands upon thousands of peer influencers.

Social-media influencers gain traction with young followers because they are young themselves, are physically attractive and have an uncanny ability to captivate and gain trust. The unfortunate reality is that these models use filters and Photoshop to present an ideal body shape and style that isn't their real body. Influencers use their popularity to advertize brand names and some influencers even get paid by retail companies just by mentioning active clothing products or by pushing certain kinds of exercise equipment. Most followers are not even aware that influencers gain a lot from their publicity on social media.

The last thing Tammy needs is to be drawn into idealized images of beauty. No one needs to be pressured by online marketers, and there is a way to get around this problem. Consider these suggestions for yourself and for the young people you care about. These recommendations will help you and your loved ones attain desired goals when it comes to fitness and anything else without being manipulated or fooled by social media:

- If you like following social media influencers, stick to positive role models. Be attracted to influencers who send the message that diversity is good, be it in body type, body weight, skin color and other traits.
- Give more attention to people both within and outside social media who tell you that your own opinion matters.

- ♎ Be careful of the motives of marketing influencers, as they don't go through the trouble of helping unless they have something to gain for themselves.
- ♎ Teach vulnerable people such as children and youth the unfortunate fact that social media pushes unrealistic bodies. When the average person cannot achieve that perfect body it is hard to resist unhealthy behaviors.

EMBRACE ALONE TIME – AGAIN AND AGAIN

Solitude is where one
discovers one is not alone.

– CANADIAN-BORN AUTHOR AND PHILOSOPHER MARTY RUBIN

Recall at the beginning I asked you to think about quarantine and its nasty effects. By looking back and comparing mandated distancing with voluntary distancing, I wanted you to sharply notice that solitude and personal space need not be all that bad. In fact, I have taken quite a strong position on the matter.

> **Having some personal space, quiet and reflection will change your mood for the better and allow you to overcome barriers and challenging times.**

To help you lead a happier and fulfilled life I asked you to face obstacles, accept challenging times and be willing to find personal space to meet your goals. This happened to my son Julian during the height of the pandemic, when he was a senior high school student. Like his high school peers Julian was required to start remote learning during the final semester of school. He expected that working without the aid of teachers or other students around him would be non-motivating and assumed he might not even pass a course or two, and he was a little nervous about the change. (In actuality, both my son and I were a tad concerned about course credit and graduation; I crossed my fingers tightly when he wasn't looking!) Luckily Julian changed his attitude and approach towards online learning and secured private workspace at home, and did a better job of organizing course materials and homework assignments. Until he started doing work from home it never dawned on him that he might actually perform better in school subjects when social and other distractions were removed. He ended up graduating. Whew!

Remember three easy steps when faced with a problem or issue and looking for new ways to meet desired goals:

- Assess the problem, including why it is present in your life at this time.
- Agree to accept circumstances that are out of your personal control.
- Find personal space and tips or strategies to meet your desired goals.

In this book I asked you to use these easy steps and boost physical exercise in the comfort of your home, add interesting and fun activities to your daily schedule, and have a go at crafting and other forms of self-expression with your hands and thinking cap. When you commit to some form of physical activity on a regular schedule the result will be that you have done something helpful for your body and you have done something to improve your emotional state. Most of all, you will have succeeded in a fitness goal, which feels nice. Activating your body and mind, in turn, will power up your self-esteem.

You have many tools available to improve your health and feel happier – and don't forget good posture and learning to be introspective, which do wonders for self-confidence and positivity.

As you work on accepting conditions that are out of your personal control it is worth saying again that you need not rely on other people to feel energized and satisfied with life. As far as lessons learned from the pandemic, I think we can agree that we do not always have people and social events to help us achieve pleasure and satisfaction, and that because of this it is paramount to learn how to achieve positive outcomes on our own.

You came across the concept of mindfulness and I offered several techniques to get you more in tune with the workings of your mind and body. Crafting a letter of gratitude, keeping a happiness journal and practicing meditation are common strategies used by therapists to help clients stay focused on the here and now while eliminating negative, automatic thinking. I asked you to use these strategies to accept present situations as they are, to stop catastrophizing and to reinterpret situations.

I hope you will give meditation a trial period to see if it works for you. Try meditation for at least one or two weeks and see if it improves your mood. Check out the assortment of guided meditation apps available, such as Headspace and Calm, which are used by many so those in particular must be good. Of course, there are many YouTube videos available depending on the type of meditation you choose. A virtual coach will guide you with step-by-step actions using a soothing and encouraging voice.

Also try sensory activities and appreciate how the senses help you navigate your world. Watch a pot of water come to a boil. Remember to record everything you hear, see, smell, feel, and taste. Eat your dinner while blindfolded and raise the value of your cuisine. Give the happiness practice a try and begin to love the small things in life, the things you ignored until now. Research shows that an exercise such as this, with journal entries made three days per week, is all you need to start changing your outlook. You will begin to view objects, people and events more positively and this in turn will produce happiness in your life, much as writing a gratitude letter to someone who means a lot to you will do. Most of all, remember that all of these activities can be done easily in the comfort and privacy of your personal space. You don't need anyone to help you stay mindful.

There are times in life when your mind will spiral out of control, when you will get anxious and afraid of things. Some people with an anxiety disorder find it difficult to control strong emotions, which gets in the way of living. You learned about distraction techniques, so use diversion methods such as listening to sounds or music, exercising, coloring, abdominal breathing and so on to lower anxiety, panic and other strong emotions. Better than that, try riding out anxiety to accept inner sensations for what they are: a normal fear response that cannot hurt you. You developed self-soothing skills to improve your emotional responses to life events – by yourself – so use them liberally.

The idea of focusing on what is happening within your body has been around for a long time. For 2,500 years (yes, that long!) Buddhist practices have involved moving attention around the body in a deliberate way, practices that originated to help people learn to accept suffering, grief and anxiety in a non-judgemental way. This is what you are doing when you ride out anxiety; that is, feeling the feelings.

Mindfulness meditation was first applied in therapy more than 30 years ago by Dr Jon Kabat-Zinn and his colleagues at the Stress Reduction Clinic at the University of Massachusetts Hospital. Their mindfulness-based stress-reduction program has helped patients with chronic pain. Less pain, anxiety and depression were found in patients who practiced regular meditation, and now mental-health practitioners teach mindfulness-based techniques so that people can learn to manage strong emotions on their own and ultimately lead a happier life.

In the feel the feelings strategy I asked you to go one step further from just being aware of what was going on inside; I asked you to better understand the meaning of your distress, why it lingers in the first place. Humans tend to misinterpret the fight/flight response as a bad reaction and try to avoid strong bodily sensations at all costs. I've done it myself many times, but never forget that the alarm system is important to every animal's survival and is adaptive. Therefore, you must learn how to interpret bodily sensations accurately and find optimal ways to handle distress. For helping me describe this process as a biologically adaptive response I give credit to the pioneering work of David Barlow and his colleagues at the Phobia and Anxiety Disorders Clinic at the University of Albany, New York.

The coronavirus pandemic caused a dramatic change in work and school life. Working from home has risen sharply since the start of the pandemic to ensure that citizens self-isolate and minimize the spread of COVID-19. Online coursework by students and webinars by adults seeking professional development also soared at the start of the pandemic. Given our changing world I have suggested strategies and materials that will help you master work and learning from the comfort of home, including:

- using sensible aids and comforting luxuries, and developing a comfortable and safe home base for doing computer and desk work
- becoming relatively cyberized and receptive to computer technology and a learning management system
- creating a work/life boundary to prevent overwork and stress
- improving time management, focus and effort, and sharpening self-learning behaviors to work independently and finish tasks.

Self-regulation skills are helpful across all domains of life, not just for doing coursework, completing webinars or doing your job. Self-regulation skills give us the chance to:

- actively take charge of activities

- reflect on how well or how poorly we are doing as far as jobs or daily tasks go
- make specific and attainable goals in order to succeed.

The running theme in this book is finding your personal space. I have referred to your private space and the need for some solitude. You have been given strategies, tips and important skills to be successful in work, school and home life. Your home space for leisure, work and school is more than just physical space; it comprises a physical location and unique domestic aids, and it consists of internal mental space for you to reflect, evaluate and make sound decisions. With personal space and solitude you can create the perfect conditions to be able to deal with challenging times.

Everyone should be prepared to tackle challenging times on their own. Remain resilient in the face of adversity. You are now empowered, and are arguably your own best advocate for living well in a changing world.

ACKNOWLEDGEMENTS

I sat down in spurts, believe it or not, over the course of three whole years and wrote this book on my own, alone – always in the presence of quiet space. I did so in front of my loyal MacBook among scattered handwritten memos, Post-it reminders, and a sizeable mug of coffee. I spent a heavenly few months at my vacation paradise in Dunedin, Florida to finish the book, in the company of sunshine, palm trees, and a long causeway for daily walking and thinking, but the ideas therein were not created unaided.

It would have been impossible to write this book and its important topics without the training I received as an impressionable student of psychology and supervisee in clinical practice. My supervisors, colleagues and comrades deserve credit for teaching me how to be a good therapist. I thank clinical psychology mentors Susan Williams and Jennifer Thomblison. It was an honor to be mentored by my doctoral thesis supervisor, Dr. Daphne Maurer, and my post-doc supervisor, Dr. Harry Shannon, from McMaster University. I appreciate the impact they made in my profession as a scholar and writer.

My ideas about how to help individuals embrace solitude for health and well-being were based on the important work of many bright theorists and dedicated researchers. My thinking was also influenced by former students and my own children. Thank you to beloved friends for encouraging me, especially over the past few years. A special thanks to Ramaswamy Venkataraman for giving my manuscript a careful reading and rereading, for offering helpful advice, and mostly for pushing me to be courageous when I most needed a lift. Thanks to my strong and smart social network of female cousins for keeping me mentally stable. (Ladies, you all know who you are!) Loyal supporters made darn sure I practiced what I preached in this self-help book.

I owe deep gratitude to Managing Director Lisa Hanrahan, who became passionate about *Alone Time* and took a chance on me. She and everyone at Rockpool Publishing got the gist of this book, especially considering a longstanding pandemic and ongoing social isolation and yet a need for voluntary distancing. I am grateful for my editors' thoughtful suggestions and feedback on content and title.

I owe the greatest debt of gratitude to the brave souls who agreed to share their trials and tribulations. My clients did this to improve the lives of others. The names and identifying information of clients in my professional practice are fictional but the issues were all real, and I hope insightful, to everyone now reading this book.

ABOUT THE
AUTHOR

ABOUT THE AUTHOR

Dr. Sybil Geldart holds a Bachelor of Arts degree from the University of Waterloo, a Master of Arts from Western University and a PhD from McMaster University in Ontario, Canada. She is an associate professor of psychology at Wilfrid Laurier University, with research interests broadly based in human development and health psychology. She has served as vice-chair of the university's Research Ethics Board, vice-chair of University Senate and assistant dean of program development in the Faculty of Human and Social Sciences.

Sybil has more than 28 years of university instructing and currently teaches in the areas of abnormal psychology, clinical psychology and special education. Outside of the university she has a part-time clinical practice and is a registered psychologist with the College of Psychologists of Ontario. She is trained in cognitive behavioral therapy and mindfulness-based therapeutic approaches for adults, adolescents and children. Both in teaching and her clinical practice, Sybil equips adults and young people with a toolbox of coping and life skills to help deal with the many stressors we all face at work and school.